The New St. Gallen Management Model

The New St. Gallen Management Model

Basic Categories of an Approach to Integrated Management

Johannes Rüegg-Stürm

© Johannes Rüegg-Stürm 2005

All rights reserved. No reproduction, copy or transmission of this publication may be made without written permission.

No paragraph of this publication may be reproduced, copied or transmitted save with written permission or in accordance with the provisions of the Copyright, Designs and Patents Act 1988, or under the terms of any licence permitting limited copying issued by the Copyright Licensing Agency, 90 Tottenham Court Road, London W1T 4LP.

Any person who does any unauthorised act in relation to this publication may be liable to criminal prosecution and civil claims for damages.

The author has asserted his right to be identified as the author of this work in accordance with the Copyright, Designs and Patents Act 1988.

First published as *Das neue St. Galler Management-Modell* by Paul Haupt Berne (2002)

First English edition published 2005 by
PALGRAVE MACMILLAN
Houndmills, Basingstoke, Hampshire RG21 6XS and
175 Fifth Avenue, New York, NY 10010
Companies and representatives throughout the world

PALGRAVE MACMILLAN is the global academic imprint of the Palgrave Macmillan division of St. Martin's Press, LLC and of Palgrave Macmillan Ltd. Macmillan® is a registered trademark in the United States, United Kingdom and other countries. Palgrave is a registered trademark in the European Union and other countries.

ISBN 1–4039–3631–5

This book is printed on paper suitable for recycling and made from fully managed and sustained forest sources.

A catalogue record for this book is available from the British Library.

Library of Congress Cataloging-in-Publication Data
Rüegg-Stürm, Johannes, 1961–
  [Neue St. Galler Management-Modell. English]
  The new St. Gallen management model: basic categories of an approach to integrated management / Johannes Rüegg-Stürm.
     p.cm.
  Includes bibliographical references and index.
  ISBN 1–4039–3631–5
  1. Industrial management. 2. Management. I. Title.

HD31.R7974 2004
658–dc22

2004050106

10 9 8 7 6 5 4 3 2 1
14 13 12 11 10 09 08 07 06 05

Printed and bound in Great Britain by
Antony Rowe Ltd, Chippenham and Eastbourne

Contents

List of Figures	vii
Preface	ix
Foreword	x

1	Introduction	1
	1.1 Structure and notes for the reader	1
	1.2 Why a management model?	2
	1.3 Theoretical basis	5
2	Firms as Complex Systems	7
	2.1 What is a complex system?	7
	2.2 Particular characteristics of the *firm* as a system	10
	2.3 Structure and overview of the basic categories of the New St. Gallen Management Model	11
3	Environmental Spheres of a Firm	14
4	The Stakeholders of a Firm	18
5	Interaction Issues Between a Firm and Its Stakeholders	21
6	Structuring Forces of a Firm	25
	6.1 Direction, coherence and shared sense of purpose	26
	6.2 Micropolitics	27
	6.3 The *strategy* of a firm	28
	6.4 Structures of a firm	34
	6.5 The culture of a firm	41
	6.6 Routinisation through structuring forces	46
7	The *Processes* of a Firm	50
	7.1 The process perspective	51
	7.2 Elements of a process	52
	7.3 Process categories	53
	7.4 Management tasks in process management	61
	7.5 Interactions between structuring forces and processes	63

8	Modes of Firm Development: *Organisational Change*	65
	8.1 Analytical–technical and cultural–relational dimension of organisational change	65
	8.2 Degree of organisational change	67
	8.3 Optimisation and renewal	68
9	Epilogue: Reinventing the Wheel?	72

Notes 77

References 81

Index 87

List of Figures

1.1	EFQM model	4
2.1	Overview of the new St. Gallen Management Model	12
3.1	Environmental spheres of a firm	14
4.1	The stakeholders of a firm	18
5.1	Interaction issues	21
6.1	Strategy, structures and culture as structuring forces of a firm	25
6.2	Strategy directs the activities of a firm	28
6.3	Content issues of a strategy	29
6.4	Development of a strategy according to the so-called Design School	32
6.5	Structures coordinate behaviour	35
6.6	Organisational chart of an aeroplane manufacturer	37
6.7	Example of a process map	38
6.8	Iterative nature of structures and processes of structuration	41
6.9	A culture creates meaning and identity	42
6.10	Circular logic of local theories and structure development	47
6.11	The organisational iceberg	47
7.1	The firm as a system of processes	50
7.2	Schematic illustration of a process-oriented firm	52
7.3	Value chain	53
7.4	Overview of the process categories	54
7.5	Management processes	56
7.6	Dimensions of management	57
7.7	Control of cycle as core leadership task of all of management processes	59
7.8	Business processes	59
7.9	Support processes	60
7.10	Circular (recursive) interaction of structuring forces and management processes	64
8.1	Analytical–technical and cultural–relational dimensions of organisational change	66
8.2	Evolutionary and revolutionary phases of firm development	68

List of Figures

8.3	Optimisation and renewal as basic modes of firm development	69
8.4	Reference points for firm development	69
9.1	Management model of the first St. Gallen Management Model and the new St. Gallen Management Model in comparison	72
9.2	The blueprint for the St. Gallen Carolingian monastery, designed and labelled around 819/830 in the Reichenau monastery	74
9.3	Reconstruction of the medieval St. Gallen monastery according to the blueprint of the St. Gallen monastery	75

Preface

Thirty-five years ago, the old business trade school in St. Gallen opened itself up to new horizons, when a group of professors and lecturers under the leadership of Hans Ulrich took a bold and decisive step away from traditional ways of teaching business management and towards an integrated approach to its delivery The 'St. Gallen Management Model' established a completely new way of training future managers, while also showing the way forward for other institutions and helping the University of St. Gallen (HSG), as it is known today, achieve an exemplary reputation of international standing.

This original St. Gallen Management Model has, even today, lost none of its attractiveness for both students and managers alike. Its clarity, its optimal simplification of complex relationships and its immediate applicability remain unequalled. There are, however, two crucial reasons for presenting additional features here. Both the practice of management and the knowledge about it have continued to develop in many ways. This must be taken into account in designing the model, without permitting faddish trends to dilute the clear basic message.

Thus on the threshold of the new century, the University of St. Gallen (HSG) undertook a fundamental reform of its system of study. On the surface, the introduction of the Anglo-Saxon Bachelor and Master system may be quite innovative. What is far more critical, however, is orienting the course towards 'head, hand and heart' (Pestalozzi) or in today's terminology 'think inter-connectedly – act professionally – convince through personality'. The new St. Gallen Management Model presented here attempts to blend these dimensions and thereby provide students with a comprehensive platform for their education. I thank Johannes Rüegg-Stürm for his commitment and overall supervision in expanding the new St. Gallen Management Model and all participating lecturers at the University of St. Gallen (HSG) for their creative involvement. Of course, I hope that the new system of study will inspire our 'HSG' (as the university is known) just as the quantum leap back then gave the impetus towards an integrated management theory.

Prof. Dr Peter Gomez
Vice-Chancellor of the University of St. Gallen

Foreword

In 1998, a group of lecturers from HSG decided to develop a framework that was to underpin a new textbook for an integrated delivery of the school's management education. It would be used as an introductory text in the newly restructured curriculum's first year of study, the so-called assessment level. This endeavour fits seamlessly into the tradition of our university. The *St. Gallen Management Model* by Hans Ulrich and Walter Krieg (1972/74) had already sprung from the desire to offer both managers and students a framework that could integrate diverse management subjects that were progressively developing into separate disciplines. This framework intended to allow complex problems to be seen in their overall context and to be dealt with effectively. By understanding management as *designing, controlling and developing purpose-oriented social institutions*, the aim was to work against a reductionist consolidation of management into a more or less random aggregation of individual disciplines. Assuming that management means primarily *mastering complexity*, an authentic approach to management was created on the basis of testing systems, and cybernetic discoveries and concepts. These insights and concepts met with great uniform resonance in both scientific discourse and in practice. This gave rise to a variety of theoretical research (for example, in St. Gallen by Gomez, 1981; Malik, 1984/2002; Probst, 1981/1987; H. Ulrich, 1978/1987 or in Munich by Kirsch, 1990), of practical applications (e.g. Gomez, 1983; Malik, 1981; H. Ulrich and Probst, 1988/2001, Gomez and Probst, 1999) and of valuable further developments (e.g. Bleicher, 1991/1999; Schwaninger, 1994).

The *St. Gallen Management Concept*, which was developed by Knut Bleicher in the second half of the 1980s and has since been constantly expanded (1991/99), forms a cornerstone of future developments. The concept is a milestone in the development of an holistic, integrated perspective on management. What is especially valuable about it is its careful differentiation between management in normative, strategic and operative dimensions.

The text presented here also lies in the tradition of HSG as a contribution to a *systems oriented management science and education*. In this sense, the new version of the St. Gallen Management Model proposed here can be considered as an organic continuation of the St. Gallen systems approach in three crucial ways:

- First, *ethical normative standards* including *social* and *ecological* responsibility now play an extraordinarily important role in businesses, as well as a careful identification and inclusion of all *stakeholders* (cf. Bleicher, 1994).
- Secondly, this text reflects the significantly increased importance of a *process-oriented perspective* of firms. On the one hand, this is due to *time-based competition* brought about through advances in information technology and, on the other hand, it is because of the increased importance of the *management of social processes*.
- This introduces the third dimension, which can be considered as an expression of an *'interpretative turn'*[1] in the social sciences. There is a growing discourse in the social sciences nowadays proceeding from the assumption that the social order (and reality) of the human world, and thus also the practice of management, is seen to be founded upon *constructing and interpretative social processes*.[2] There is an attempt to explain this order through careful contextual analyses of complex communicative and relational processes. In the study of management, this interpretative turn is expressed in themes such as *corporate culture* or *symbolic management* – and it is precisely in *change management*, where the implementation of these phenomena significantly determines success or failure.

This text also embodies the framework of the new management studies textbook (Dubs *et al.*, 2004), which is already being used as an instruction tool in the new *assessment level* (the first year of study) at HSG. In this sense, the observations made here provide a short, introductory overview of the *basic categories of an integrated management education* within an overall context for the manager and student.

I would like to thank sincerely everyone who has provided me with valuable ideas and constructive criticism. During the stage of conception, these people were, in particular, *Rolf Dubs, Peter Gomez, Georg von Krogh, Günter Müller-Stewens, Markus Schwaninger* and *Emil Walter-Busch*. During the stage of realisation, *Dieter Euler, Christina Wyss, Matthias von der Heyden, Hans Seitz, Peter Staub* and *Christian Erk* – authors of the many management studies textbook and students from the first generation of our newly restructured curriculum – have given a great deal of assistance.

I would like to give special thanks to both *Peter Gomez*, for his friendly preface and for his untiring support for the entire textbook project, and to my colleague *Peter Ulrich*, who has repeatedly analysed the whole text critically and constructively, and has provided me with extremely important and valuable inputs concerning both the methodology and terminology I have used.

Christina Wyss, doctoral candidate and research associate at the University of St. Gallen (HSG) has greatly contributed to the editing of the final versions of this translation. In cooperation with *Sally Gschwend-Fisher* and *Dominik Reichenmiller*, they cautiously considered the different cultural contexts of language in translation. As a wide range of management science can be considered to be a hermeneutic discipline, this involves transforming implicitly held, yet interconnected assumptions from the German into the Anglo-Saxon culture. I want to sincerely thank *Christina Wyss*, *Sally Gschwend-Fisher* and *Dominik Reichenmiller* for their excellent work. Last but not least, I am deeply grateful to *Nicole Weber*. Her highly competent project management combined with her charming esteem contributed continuously and profoundly to the successful completion of this task.

University of St. Gallen
Johannes Rüegg-Stürm

1
Introduction

1.1 Structure and notes for the reader

This first chapter will discuss fundamental aspects about the reason and purpose for a management model and provide a short overview of the theoretical basis for this text. The second chapter reveals our underlying perception that firms can be conceptualised by means of six fundamental descriptive dimensions (basic categories). The following chapters will examine the individual basic categories in more detail.

Important conceptual terms appear in blue – these terms are listed in alphabetical order in the index. The page reference in the index indicates where in the book certain terms are explained in detail. If you encounter an unfamiliar term a glance in the index should prove helpful.

1.2 Why a management model?

We are all used to models, particularly in the natural sciences. In scientific models, hypothetical causal relationships are depicted mathematically, then tested and verified in demanding experiments.

Architects, designers and geographers also use models. Such physical models serve to illustrate complicated relationships. The model of an architect or a designer allows clients to evaluate the building project or the relevance of important materials before they are realised. A topographical model helps understand a mountainous region in terms of its structural formation and origin.

Closely related to such models are maps. Every map is based on *signatures* that represent certain aspects of the depicted terrain. Signatures do not, therefore, have anything to do with the terrain itself, rather are *constructed, commonly agreed symbols, signs and definitions*. They serve the *reconstruction* of a terrain with respect to *successfully fulfilling specific purposes*. To this end, the following aspects are particularly important:

- Maps do not specify what we must do. They provide no formulae. We must decide ourselves which route or other course to follow. A map adapted to the problem at hand can facilitate this process.
- The symbols used in a map depend upon the *purpose* of the map. A hydrological or a climatic map is based on signatures different from those of a hiking map.
- A map never represents a terrain, rather, it is a *reconstruction* of this terrain according to the purpose and task of the map. The pivotal function of a map exists in highlighting important things and leaving out less important things – or, in other words: in its *reduction of complexity*. With a little exaggeration, it can be said that the usefulness of a map exists in what it omits. Our world is almost infinitely complex. To act in a time-efficient manner requires disregarding purposefully certain factors so that complexity is reduced. In other words, the challenge is to decide only *once* – and not over and over again – what is, or is not, important in any given context for similar demands and problems.
- Our world is not only infinitely complex but it is also infinitely huge. Drawing a map requires not only choosing appropriate signatures but also *fixing the region to be covered by the map* and, thereby, determining its scale. Every map delineates implicitly the borders of

its perceived problems (problem definition) thus separating whatever deserves attention from that which lies outside the scope of the problem.
- From the customer's point of view, therefore, 'the one' map does not exist. We have to rather select a map according to our goals and the tasks that we need to accomplish. When we are driving along in our cars, we need a comparatively large-scale street atlas. In stark contrast to this is orienteering, where we have to locate a well-hidden post in a hollow in the ground or when we have to search for a tricky way down hills.
- As a consequence, there are neither right nor wrong maps but, rather, maps that are more or less appropriate or inappropriate according to specific contexts and tasks. Of course, in terms of correct signatures or scale, maps can be misleading when, for example, roads and streets have been incorrectly entered or even omitted completely.

Our Management Model shares many similarities with an orienteering map for examining management. What purpose could a model, in the sense of an orienteering map, have in the context of management?

1. As linguistic, often graphically illustrated constructions, models help us to differentiate swiftly between *what is important from what is less important*. They contain, however, no instruction manual or even formulae.
2. A model forms a *framework*, illustrating logical and specific *causal relationships* between significant factors, thus promoting speedy orientation (in terms of 'sensemaking') in situations of high uncertainty and ambiguity. This will be demonstrated with reference to a management model and specifically to its pivotal role in Quality Management, the so-called EFQM Model of the European Foundation for Quality Management (EFQM 2002).
   The model's nine criteria help in assessing the development of all types of organisations (companies, authorities, schools, social institutions, etc.) as they progress towards top performance. The assessment model focuses on success and takes equal account of initial steps toward quality improvement ('enablers') and of the achievements already reached. The careful scrutiny of financial figures forms just one part of a more comprehensive goal-orientation. Financial figures are considered as more of a symptom than a cause. Therefore,

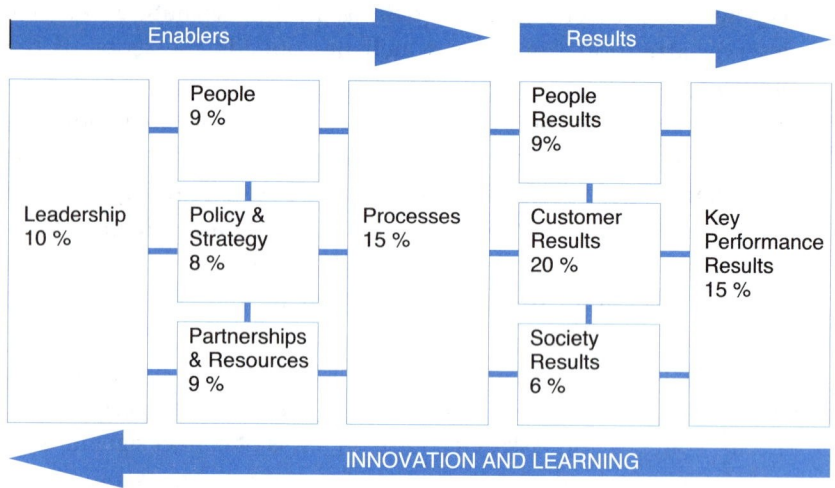

Figure 1.1 EFQM model

the criteria of *people results* (in particular employee satisfaction), *customer results* (in particular customer satisfaction) and *society results* (in particular image) with their collective 35 per cent are weighted far more heavily than an organisation's financial key performance results with 15 per cent.
3. Just as with every management concept and leadership tool, a model helps in *structuring organisational communication*. It serves especially in *directing focus*, inasmuch as it repeatedly steers leadership focus towards specific phenomena. Thus, there are business managers who structure their meetings according to the categories of the EFQM Model insofar as at each stage of the EFQM Model they ask the question: how or through which causal relationship[3] does our work as managers influence the results of the firm?
4. As a linguistic construction in common usage – in the sense of a common language, a common discourse, a common way of looking at the work of the management – a model facilitates speedier understanding. This strengthens an organisation's *collective ability to act*.
5. In terms of modern linguistic understanding,[4] categorical models do not normally represent reality; rather, they create *reality only in triggering processes of collective sensemaking*. With the help of language (and linguistic coordination), a certain linguistic tradition (dis-

course) is crystallised through a common approach to overcoming everyday demands. Inextricably linked to this, moreover, is a common basis for thought and reason, upon which a meaningful framework can be built for fulfilling further challenges.[5] Without commonly employed and intelligently understood terms, i.e. without 'discursive resources', we can neither describe nor comprehend anything. In this sense, language precedes reality and is an unavoidable prerequisite for every form of understanding. Thus, for example, we can only concern ourselves with competitive strategies (of rivals) when we have access to the appropriate concepts, and the appropriate discourses are recognised in both theory and practice. Competitive strategies can only ever evolve at all, however, *precisely because* appropriate concepts and discourses develop, find resonance in the practice of management, are applied to practical decisions and thereby spread. Understanding language in this way, models have to some extent adopted the character of 'self-fulfilling prophecies'.

In the following text, models are, therefore, to be understood as contingent inventions, *illustrating a range of actions considered to be significant* and *postulating specific causal relationships*. 'Something which is contingent is neither necessary nor impossible; it is something which can exist as it does…, but which is also possible in other forms' (Luhmann, 1984, p. 152). As contingent constructions models can break down and fail. An unavoidable *blind spot* is created when models fulfil their goal exactly by taking no account of unimportant matters and purposefully omitting certain factors in an essential reduction of complexity. Models represent a serious risk if, despite this uncertain background, they feign a false reliability. In this sense, models embody nothing more or nothing less than useful, contingent intellectual maps, which over the course of time and through the repeated fulfilment of more or less similar tasks undergo constant re-examination and improvement.

1.3 Theoretical basis

As already outlined in the Foreword, this text is primarily based upon the theoretical work on the systems approach introduced by Hans Ulrich and his colleagues from the University of St. Gallen (HSG). Other significant intellectual stimuli which have influenced this text from an epistemological and social-scientific point of view are Niklas Luhman's *Sociological Theory of Systems* (1984), Anthony Giddens' *theory of structuration* (1984), and *perspectives on social constructionism* of applied social sciences (Dachler, 1990, 1992; Burr, 1995; Hosking *et al.*, 1995; Gergen, 1999). Of equal importance from an ethical and normative point of view is the approach towards *integrated ethics in economy and business* by Peter Ulrich (2001). If one attempted to subsume all of these theoretical intellectual headings under one phrase, one could propose a *systemic-constructionist approach to management*, the roots for which had already been firmly established by Hans Ulrich (H. Ulrich and Probst, 1984).

2
Firms as Complex Systems

Our perception of firms is, to a large extent, shaped by *fundamental precepts of systems theory*.[6] In other words, a firm is understood to be a complex system in our model. By a system, we mean an *ordered entirety* of *elements*. A system becomes *complex*, when the elements of a system *interact* in a variety of ways and interrelate with each other in a specific and dynamic *relationship*. This theoretical description will be explained thoroughly in the ensuing text.

2.1 What is a complex system?

2.1.1 Systems and the environment

First and foremost, a system is an *entirety* of elements, an *integrated whole*, a *unity* which is *distinguishable* from its environment. The ability to distinguish implies that there must be recognisable *borders* which allow a firm to set itself apart from its environment. There are a variety of criteria for such separation and many types of borders. For example, there are institutional borders such as membership (having a contract of employment with the firm) or borders of identity (a sense of belonging and considering oneself to be a part of the firm), etc. Demarcating the borders of a firm, i.e. defining a firm as a unity (or entity) in a complex environment, is no trivial matter in light of the increasingly diverse terms of contract and the enormous number of different forms of cooperation undertaken by today's firms with others (customers, suppliers, partners).

2.1.2 Systems and *system elements*

A system is a unity comprising *elements*. Elements are the *components* of a system – everything which constitutes an *interconnecting* system. However, elements should not exclusively refer to *material* or *object-like* elements such as buildings, furnishings, machines, infrastructures of communication technology or information technology, products, documents, artefacts and employees. At least of equal importance are *immaterial* elements too, those having no objective physical embodiment such as events, patterns of communication, relationships, processes, teams, departments, divisions, principles of conduct, strategies, etc.

2.1.3 Interconnection and dynamism as expressions of system complexity

The *diversity* of the elements and of the *interactions* between these elements forms the *complexity* of a system. We describe a system as *complex* when:

- multiple and not easily intelligible relationships and interactions between the elements of a system exist;
- due to various *reconnections* and a certain *independence inherent* in the system elements these relationships and interactions undergo *constant and barely predictable change*; and
- these relationships and interactions, or the way in which the *system behaves*, provide *emergent* results, i.e. results that can in *no* possible way be traced back to peculiarities or characteristics of *individual* elements; rather, they arise from ways in which the elements of the system *combine* and especially in the dynamics of their interaction. This means the results depend upon certain *patterns* of recurring interactions that emerged historically.

Therefore, complex systems are typically *dynamic systems*, meaning that they are constantly developing, are in constant 're-construction'.

2.1.4 Implications of system complexity

These dynamics inherent in complex systems impede appreciating fully a specific complex system from a central point, to *describe* it completely and 'objectively' and to represent it 'exactly' in a model.[7]

The way *(how)* we describe a complex system depends, firstly, on the scale of our mental viewfinder and, specifically, on the available 'signatures' and terms, or in other words, on the *linguistic possibilities* (discursive resources) which we have at our disposal for descriptions.

Secondly, how we describe a system and thus how we perceive a business problem depends crucially on the *context within which we interpret what we are observing*. Whether we see the glass on the table as either half full or half empty depends on how thirsty we are (context). Whether we attribute certain events and consequences to a different cause and chain of events than our political opponents depends on our political affiliation, etc.

Thus, complexity always implies that the observation and interpretation of events within and around firms is inevitably *selective*, bound up with *contingent acts of selection* (Luhmann, 1984). The light in which a firm and its problems appear, depends on the context and the perspective which have arisen from these acts of selection (Morgan, 1997). These different appearances give rise to varying ways of looking at problems and to varying focus areas for a company leadership's work activities.

Such an approach to management reveals clearly two things: first, we can predict the behaviour of complex systems only to a very limited degree (a similar problem arises with the weather forecast, too). Secondly, the spheres of influence exercised by the management, that is everything concerning the governance, design, control and development of a firm (H. Ulrich, 1984), are clearly bounded. There are strict limits to the creativity within management and the ability to shape an organisation because firms are entirely different constructions than machine-like, technologically alterable devices such as cars, where the control and absolute reliability of continuous processes (steering, braking, acceleration, etc.) are the paramount requirements of such a vehicle's usefulness.

2.1.5 Order of a system

Looking at it from a different angle, however, the variety of relationships, interactions and exchanges within a firm do not in any way imply that complex systems are completely arbitrary, i.e. events within are chaotic and unpredictable. If a system were like this, then it would promptly fail and dissolve into nothingness. In such conditions, every form of cooperation and division of labour would be fundamentally impossible. For complex systems to remain viable, therefore, they are compelled to rely upon *structuring influences* and *ordering forces*. This explains precisely why *leadership*, regardless of whom or how, is absolutely necessary.

Structures evolve in complex systems through *repeatedly similar executions of processes*. They reveal themselves in *patterns* of interaction and communication, in the development of mutual *expectations* (roles), etc. which after time have a certain constancy and stability. Just as complex systems are characterised through the particular ways in which labour is divided, they are also characterised by a certain degree of *order* (Probst, 1987), through *repeatedly emerging patterns* in *day-to-day communication, decision-making, leadership* and *cooperation*. Patterns in day-to-day events express the predominant order created through these processes of *structuration*[8] (the formation of order).

2.2 Particular characteristics of the *firm* as a system

Firms (business firms) manifest a host of particular characteristics which set them apart from other complex systems (P. Ulrich & Fluri, 1995, p. 31):

- They are *economic* systems, which mean that, in the long run, the financial revenues of a firm must cover the expenditure incurred from the current consumption of resources.
- Firms are *purpose-oriented* and are *multi-functional*. This means they must perform *functions for other systems* through their own specific value creation and, thereby, satisfy the demands of *several* stakeholders at once.
- Firms are *socio-technical systems*. United in different 'communities-of-practice'[9] and supported by technical means, people fulfil certain tasks to the benefit of their stakeholders, in a highly complicated process based on the division of labour.

Additionally, firms are in *economic competition* with other business firms. From an economic point of view, the rules of this competition are to *remove shortages* with the least amount of resources and to *create new shortages* through the creative discovery and invention of new needs and demands. Thus, in constant competition, the only firms tasting success will be those able to discover time and again new business opportunities which create value, and be able to exploit those opportunities better than their competitors. In other words, they will enjoy a comparably *superior value creation* for the different stakeholders (advantage of effectiveness) and operate at *lower costs* (advantage of efficiency). With the right effort a firm will ideally maintain a sustainable competitive advantage.

2.3 Structure and overview of the basic categories of the new St. Gallen Management Model

On the basis of the terms outlined above, we can distinguish between six central descriptive categories in the new St. Gallen Management Model:

- environmental spheres
- stakeholders
- interaction issues
- structuring forces
- processes
- modes of development.

These so-called basic categories relate to the inner dimensions of management. In contrast to Anglo-Saxon countries, we mean by management neither the less attractive administrative part of leadership, nor a group of executives in the sense of 'the' management of company X has decided on Y or Z. In the German speaking context, leadership is, in general, narrower conceptualised in terms of *leading people,* whereas management is understood as a basic function or as a system of complex tasks which Hans Ulrich (1984) has well summarised as *designing, controlling and further developing purpose-oriented socio-technical organisations.*[10]

The main focus of business activities is dependent upon environmental spheres. Depending on the industry or area of business activity, these environmental spheres must take stock of important trends that lead to change.

12 | The New St. Gallen Management Model

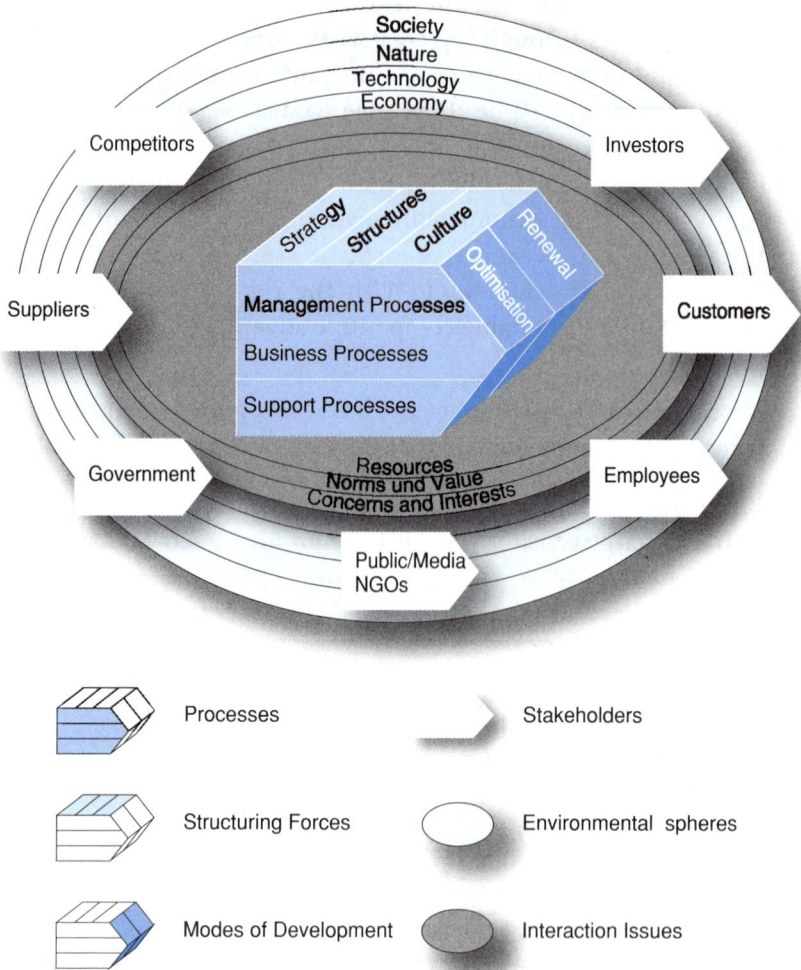

Figure 2.1 Overview of the new St. Gallen Management Model[11]

Stakeholders are organised or not-organised groups of people, organisations and institutions, which are affected by the company's value-creating activities and sometimes also by value-destroying activities.

The 'issues' in the relationship between stakeholders and businesses define the **interaction issues**. The manner in which the firm communicates with its stakeholders depends upon these **issues**. Thus, on the one hand, we can identify personal and cultural elements such as concerns, interests, norms and values and, on the other hand, material elements, such as resources. Interaction issues, then, are partly bound up with a discussion of issues and partly about tradeable goods and rights. In short, interaction issues denote the various issues in the communicative processes with the stakeholders.

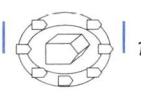

A firm's value-added activities are not decided randomly, rather, they run to a more or less ordered course – even when the corresponding patterns of communication and activity are usually difficult to recognise (reconstruct). Structuring forces[12] lend to the day-to-day organisational issues a more coherent form, imposing upon them a certain order and thus orientating these daily issues towards the accomplishment of particular effects and results.

All of a firm's value-added activities and necessary work required by the management team to fulfil them, are achieved through processes. These processes are characterised by a certain functional and sequential logic as specific tasks are executed.

Human curiosity and creativity, in general, and innovative companies, in particular, have a decisive involvement in generating strong dynamics in their environment. These dynamics make it vital for every firm to continue developing. The modes of development describe fundamental patterns in how firms sustain development.

In the following chapters, these basic categories are described in detail.

3
Environmental Spheres of a Firm

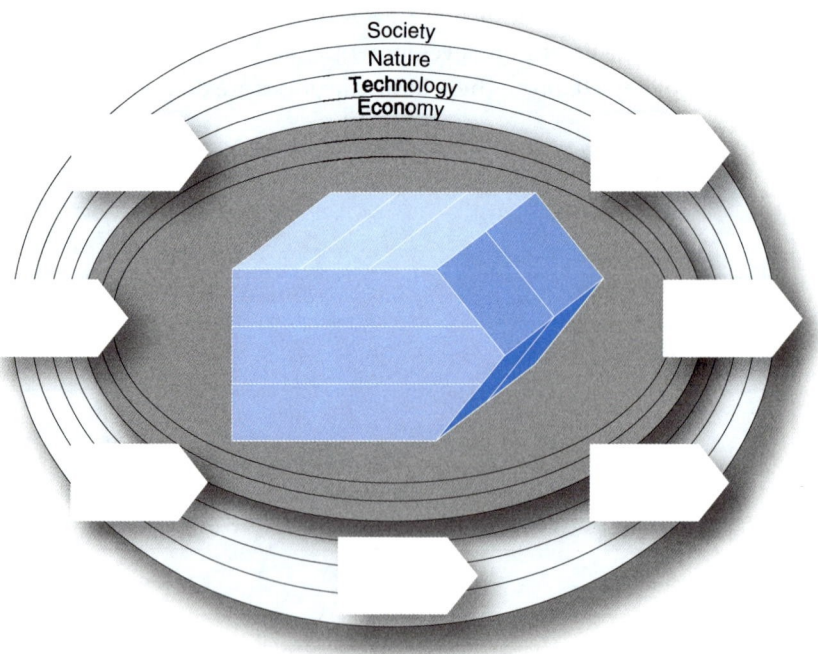

Figure 3.1   Environmental spheres of a firm

In the new St. Gallen Management Model, we distinguish among four important environmental spheres. The most all-encompassing sphere is society. It is the *social discourse* which impacts upon how nature as such is actually perceived, how technological developments progress, and how economic value creation should occur. With respect to the environmental sphere *society*, for example, firms might be interested in the following aspects and their related trends:

- the population's readiness to work and the level of education;
- the population's open-mindedness towards unfamiliar and new ideas;
- the population's willingness to take risks;
- the population's age structure;
- the distribution of income and wealth;
- social problems and potential for conflict;
- the role of the government and the manner in which public opinion is shaped;
- political culture and limiting conditions;
- political forces;
- public infrastructure and educational opportunities;
- …

The environmental sphere *nature* is not simply – as one might believe – of a given magnitude. One's perception and opinion of the *environmental sphere nature* depends crucially upon current social discourses. With controversial ecological concerns in particular, these discourses can differ dramatically according to country, culture and the social and economic context within which they take place. This is especially important for globally active companies. The following aspects, for example, might be of particular interest for firms:

- abundance of resources (air, water, surface area, mineral resources and raw materials)
- access to the ocean
- agricultural potential
- topography
- climate (temperature, humidity, daily and seasonal patterns)
- biological diversity (flora and fauna)
- pollution
- …

The environmental sphere *technology* is heavily influenced by social discourses, for example, in the perception of risk. It is also, however, closely linked to economic forces. Technological developments are important to companies in the following areas:

- biological and genetic engineering
- process engineering
- material technology
- energy production technology
- traffic technology
- communication and information technology
- ...

In addition to these and other technologies, however, what kind of *enabling conditions* for technology development are provided is also important. Thus, locations have arisen which represent a growing dynamic force of progress in particular fields on the strength of the proximity and density of related centres of development and associated investments. These include Silicon Valley in the field of semiconductor technology, the Bay Area (USA), Boston (USA), Cambridge (UK) and Martinsreid/Munich or the Rhineland (Germany) in the field of biological and chemical engineering. Firms would, therefore, do well to take heed of not only technological developments as such but also of the structure of these geographical *technology clusters*.

The environmental sphere *economy* with its procurement, commercial, labour, and financial markets is to a certain extent the very breeding ground of a firm, upon which a sustainable interdependent relationship should be established. The following aspects might be of particular importance in this sphere:

- macroeconomic structures
- access to procurement and commercial markets
- efficiency of labour and financial markets, availability of capital
- concentration of suppliers and customers
- traffic infrastructure
- telecommunications infrastructure
- ...

These examples, too, illustrate that the development of the economy is closely related to complex social and political processes.

Finally, it must be mentioned that dividing a company's environment into four spheres should by no means give the impression that there are clearly identifiable categories. It is not easy to discern whether, for example, developments in intellectual property law should belong to the environmental sphere *society* (influence of NGOs in political opinion-forming), the environmental sphere *technology* (the implications of patenting life itself for the future development of biological and genetic engineering) or *economy* (the migration of suppliers, partners and customers to countries with 'pro-business' legislation). In other words, environmental spheres merely provide an analytical guidebook to identify trends which are critical for success.

4
The Stakeholders of a Firm

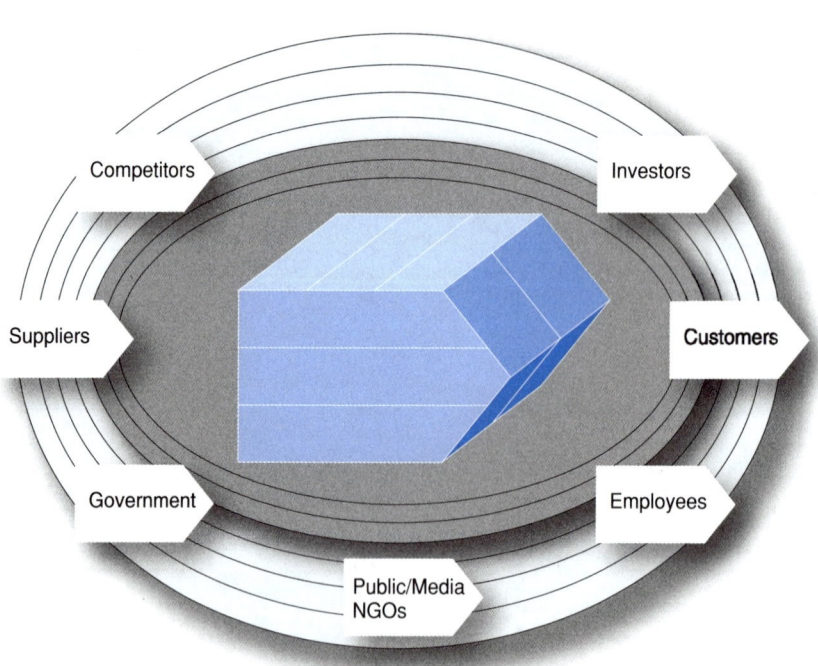

Figure 4.1   The stakeholders of a firm

A firm is never a means to its own end, rather, it must realise its business activities, which must provide a social benefit in active interaction with the most varied of **stakeholders**. These are represented in the outermost circle of the Management Model. On the left-hand side are stakeholders who provide the operating conditions or the resources. On the right-hand side are stakeholders who, in most cases, are relatively directly and deeply affected by the company's value creation. Fundamental to the relationship with all stakeholders is the attempt to establish a fair balance of give and take.

The illustration should not, however, give rise to the impression that it is universally valid or final.

In the first instance, firms must give thorough consideration to the groups of people, organisations and institutions which will be affected by or included in the firm's value creation or value destruction.

Secondly, after each individual group has been identified, it must be examined, rethought and redefined in the light of further complexities. Thus, the stakeholders mentioned in the illustration might need to be redefined according to their context so that in Switzerland, for example, the stakeholder 'government' needs to be broken down into the federal, cantonal, and municipal level, while the stakeholder 'public' can be divided into neighbours, individual environmental organisations, and so on.

Thirdly, the reasoning for this choice can arise either from a strategic stakeholder value approach, or from an ethically critical stakeholder approach (cf. in detail P. Ulrich, 2001, pp. 438ff.). Both of these approaches are based on ideal–typical regulative schools of thought, which will now be briefly described:

- The *Strategic Stakeholder Value Approach* (Freeman, 1984) bases the selection of appropriate stakeholders primarily on the *impact* of their concerns, interests and demands in *securing the future* of a firm – those who, perhaps due to having the power of disposal over limited resources or the power of sanction, can influence the long or short term viability of a firm. The strategic management of stakeholders, then, is expressed ideal-typically in maintaining the willingness of all participants to cooperate and in *securing the agreement (goodwill)* of influential stakeholders.
- The *Ethically Critical Stakeholder Value Approach* (P. Ulrich, 2001, pp. 442f.) acknowledges fundamentally all people impacted positively

or negatively by the firm's actions as appropriate stakeholders, since their humanity entitles them to dignity and moral rights (for example, children without a lobby), *irrespective* of their influence, power, or position. The relevant criterion here is not the impact of stakeholder concerns, but solely the *ethically justifiable legitimacy* of the stated interests. An ethically critical management of stakeholders is then concerned primarily with *consensus-oriented resolutions of conflicts of interest*[13] and with carefully and ethically balancing and legitimising interests by assuming, in a sense, the role of a respectful, impartial, responsible world citizen.

What often arises in practice is a combination of these two regulative schools of thought, or stakeholder value approaches.

In contrast to our understanding of a consensus-based approach to business management, (neoliberal) followers of the so-called *Shareholder Value Approach* hold the utilitarian belief that a firm's social responsibility is confined to maximising profit.[14] This school of thought argues that – within legal limits – a free, transparent, and efficient market, guided by the *invisible hand* (Adam Smith), will automatically lead to the maximisation of public welfare and thus to an optimal satisfaction of stakeholder demands. Of course, this viewpoint precludes the necessity for a systematic management of stakeholders.

The *Stakeholder Value Approach* (in the sense of the *strategic* stakeholder value approach already outlined) is a watered down version of the Shareholder Value Approach. It argues that is precisely by striving towards a *long-term balanced consideration of all stakeholders* that maximum shareholder value is inevitably achieved. This (normative) perspective is countered by the idea that ethically justifiable and morally imperative decisions can arise which favours certain stakeholders while foregoing any long-term positive impact on shareholder value. This implies the investors consciously ignoring their own interests in favour of those of other stakeholders.[15]

5
Interaction Issues between a Firm and Its Stakeholders

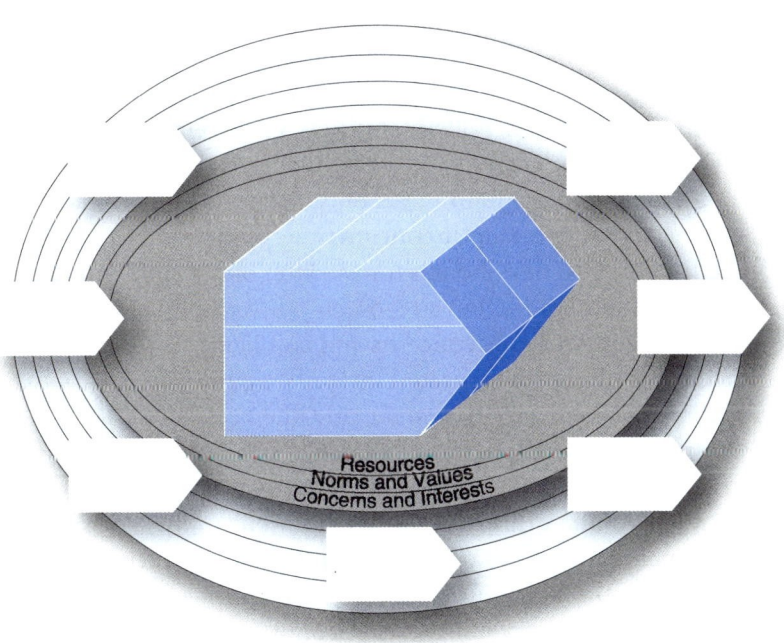

Figure 5.1 Interaction issues

A whole variety of commercial relationships occur between a firm and its stakeholders. In addition, there is normally an 'issue' in these relationships over which the parties contend with varying vigour.[16] The nature of these *'issues'* can be more *ideal* and *intangible*, or *material* and *tangible* in the sense of commercial and disposable goods and rights.

Interaction issues take up a position in the inner circle of the Management Model between the environmental spheres and the firm. They refer to *what* stakeholders bring to the company, what they give the company access to, or what of the company they dispute. From a different perspective, interaction issues refer to *the issues which* a firm must tackle. A distinction is to be made between intangible *personal* and *cultural* elements such as *concerns, interests, norms* and *values*, on the one hand, and *tangible* (material) elements such as *resources*, on the other hand.[17]

As already explained in Chapter 4, the people, organisations or institutions bounded up with a firm are to be counted among its stakeholders if they are *affected* by the business activity directly or indirectly, whether through benefits, risks, or the short-term or long-term promotion or limitation of their quality of life or potential for development. Thus, stakeholders can assume *demands* from the environmental spheres *society, technology, nature* and *economy* and assert their interests by realising these demands.

To fulfil our ideal of a holistic business management, a normative –critical and ethical concept of stakeholders requires that different stakeholders' concerns and interests must each time be *carefully considered and evaluated*. Whether it concerns the production of genetically modified organisms, new models for working hours and remuneration or the closure of a production site – such projects frequently engender controversial demands, i.e. concerns and conflicting interests. To carry out such plans, these concerns and interests require *respectful consideration and carefully reasoned evaluation*, and the *explanation* for the final decision must be *understood (legitimisation)*.

Thus at certain times, *norms* and *values* play an important social role. These moral norms and values, as well as the decisions and actions which a firm bases on them, require constant *ethical reflection* and *legitimisation*. It is not achieving short-term market success or maintaining long-term viability which should form the only *guiding principle* for legitimising business activities. Rather, in terms of *normative management*, strategic and operative decision-making processes should be firmly based upon ethical considerations.[18] On the other hand, however, a society's prevailing norms and values are also heavily influenced by business' legitimisation and decision-making processes.

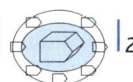

Nevertheless, these legitimisation and decision-making processes provide companies not only with a specific *normative frame of reference*, but also with a specific access to what are often limited and sometimes highly controversial *resources* – resources which are vital and are readily used in a firm's value creation process. Indeed, what can be considered *legitimate and useful resources*, the resources actually available (e.g. raw materials, energy, land, patent rights, finances, labour,[19] knowledge, genomes of plants, animals or even people) to a firm for specific circumstances (considering the price, quality and condition when used) depend crucially upon the *prevailing norms and values*. These norms and values may give rise to *inherent disputes* over the *principles guiding* the company's activities, and this also plays a part in considering resources. Resources, therefore, take up the innermost position in the inner circle.

To summarise, then, a firm's environment comprises *stakeholders* who represent their *concerns* and *interests* against the background of certain *norms* and *values*. Ideally, *arguments are discussed fairly* and a *normative agreement* follows which decisively influences which activities and procedures a firm should pursue (or avoid) in principle and also which *resources* a firm aims to acquire for the purpose of its economic value creation.

Based upon an ideally consensus-based normative frame of reference, companies must carry out a workable *strategic positioning* within the web of stakeholder relationships. To do this, companies primarily follow the *economic logic of the market*, or business opportunities. This means that firms *selectively* take up certain concerns, interests, needs and demands of specific stakeholders, *prioritise* appropriately, and then use this to outline *strategic directions, goals, initiatives* and *projects*.

By using or developing the widest variety of technologies possible, these strategic directions and goals must be translated into *effective* and *efficient value creation processes for a company*. In order to understand this particular challenge properly, we must examine the 'fabric' of a firm more closely. This should facilitate a better understanding of how a modern business operates within the context of *market logic*.

The following considerations are, therefore, based less on a normative–critical, ethical perspective but more on a *strategic–functional* one: how should we picture the 'operation' of a complex modern organisation such as a business firm within the context of a competitive market logic? How is a company's conduct made cohesive and effective, and which areas of responsibility for the company's leaders arise from this?

6
Structuring Forces of a Firm

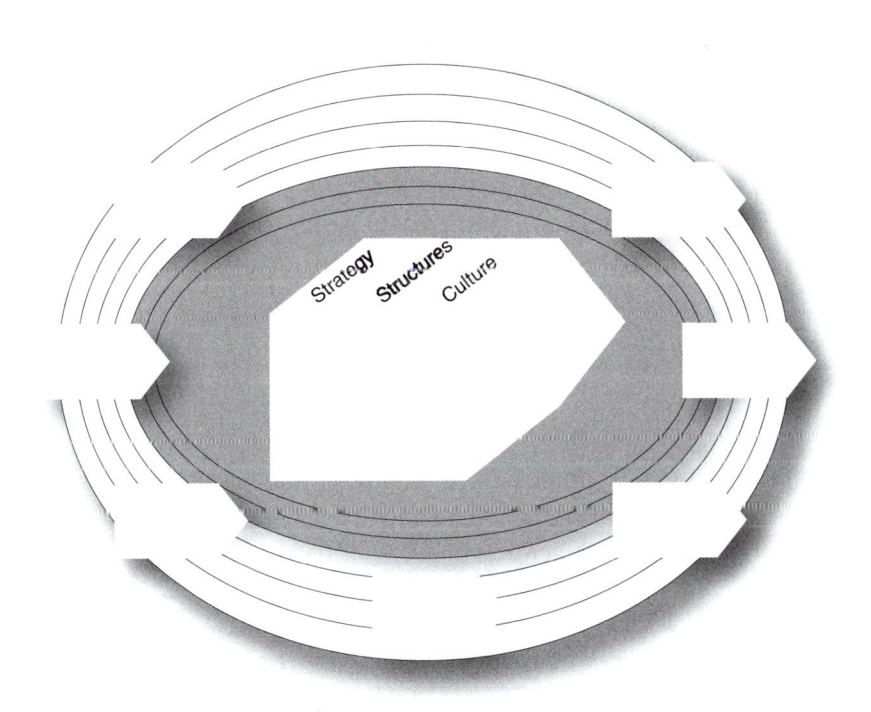

Figure 6.1 Strategy, structures and culture as structuring forces of a firm

6.1 Direction, coherence and shared sense of purpose

If firms are to remain *viable* in an economic sense, i.e. creating superior benefits for the stakeholders in an efficient and lasting manner, then they must fulfil three criteria.[20]

In the first instance, a firm must always develop new strategic *orientation knowledge* which ensures that all of its efforts and endeavours work towards fulfilling those aspects by which it measures success. More simply put, it is about ensuring that WHAT is done is in each case the *right* thing to do.[21] This *directional function* is based upon a workable orientation plan and it forms the firm's business *strategy*.

The long-term success of any business activity does not only depend upon skilfully directing the processes of value creation but also upon a high degree of *coherence* and *fine-tuning* of all business activities. The necessary coherence and fine-tuning demand *coordination*, or a variety of carefully correlated mechanisms. Simply put, it is about HOW things are done – that 'things are done *right*.' This *coordinating function*, based upon a workable strategy, is provided by the *structures* of a firm.

In unforeseen events, each member of the company must be able to act and react according to a common *sense of purpose* that goes beyond the strategic and structural arrangements of the company. Stated differently, this sense of purpose provides answers to questions of WHY and WHAT FOR. This sense of purpose can, for example, be expressed in a workable, implied, or even explicitly formulated vision and in an agreed upon collective identity. In a firm, a shared sense of purpose fulfils several important functions related to creating a *healthy social environment, successful cooperation* and *economic success*:[22]

- No company can ever ensure that every detail is clearly and completely governed by strategic and structural stipulations. On the contrary, in a dynamic environment this would cause companies to jam immediately and spell their certain end. People must, therefore, be able to *interpret rules with a degree of flexibility* and, remaining within the business activity as a whole, also act within a 'deregulated' sphere. We could describe this as the *confidence function*: 'What gives us the confidence to act appropriately within the firm as a whole, even if there are no clear regulations available.'

- This sense of purpose must also provide an anchor when people are required to understand and organise ambiguous or even contradictory (paradoxical) events quickly and appropriately. We could describe this as the *sensemaking function* (Weick, 1979): 'What enables us to make sense of highly ambiguous and contradictory events and to organise them appropriately in a coherent framework.'
- A shared sense of purpose must help to enthuse people about the business activity or at least help to develop a minimum of motivation, identification and inner energy for these activities. We could describe this as the *motivational function*: 'Why we are happy to work here.'

To summarise, then, the general sense of purpose fulfils in many ways the *function of creating meaning* for a firm. It is embodied to a considerable extent by the *culture* of a firm (P. Ulrich, 1984).

6.2 Micropolitics

Strategy, structures and culture do not at all arise solely from purely factual, logical, rational considerations in the way towards a (fictional) common interest. Whenever people are working closely with others, there will always be issues of *self-interest* and *power* because everyone, whether working as an individual or as a representative of specific stakeholders and coalitions, will pursue personal agendas. Fuelling these personal agendas is the desire to fulfil life-long individual goals (Watson, 1994), or even, for stakeholders, the desire to achieve institutionalised goals (Dyllick, 1989). *Micropolitical processes of negotiation*,[23] therefore, dictate the development of a strategy, of structures, of a culture, and also the development of individual goals, which the individual processes of a firm aim to fulfil. All those impacted by these processes – inasmuch as they can influence such negotiations – have their own agendas, argue for the legitimacy of the demands, wrestle for acceptance and also form coalitions to represent their interests if necessary. This causes leading groups (or clans) to arise. Out of all of the groups, the leading group can be understood as the 'dominant coalition' of a firm and thus enjoys increased influence over the direction of strategic goals and structures as well as the expression of the culture (Kieser, 1998).

6.3 The *strategy* of a firm

6.3.1 Definition and tasks

Management tasks in a firm can be dedicated to one of two intrinsically different duties: on the one hand, the immediate *carrying out of everyday business activities*, i.e. negotiating contracts and projects, and, on the other hand, *creating the prerequisites* that allow businesses to achieve *long-term economic success*. While the former is concerned with success in the here and now, the latter endeavours to achieve success in a time horizon of three, five or ten years.

Strategic management concerns itself with systematically examining the *foundations for long-term success* of a firm. A strategy is drawn up during demanding negotiations and decision-making processes, taking account of needs, concerns, interests, demands and moral values of all of the stakeholders, whether they are actively taking part in the processes or will be affected by them. There are two important aspects to a strategy:

First of all, a strategy must provide *detailed* information about the following five areas (cf. Fig. 8)

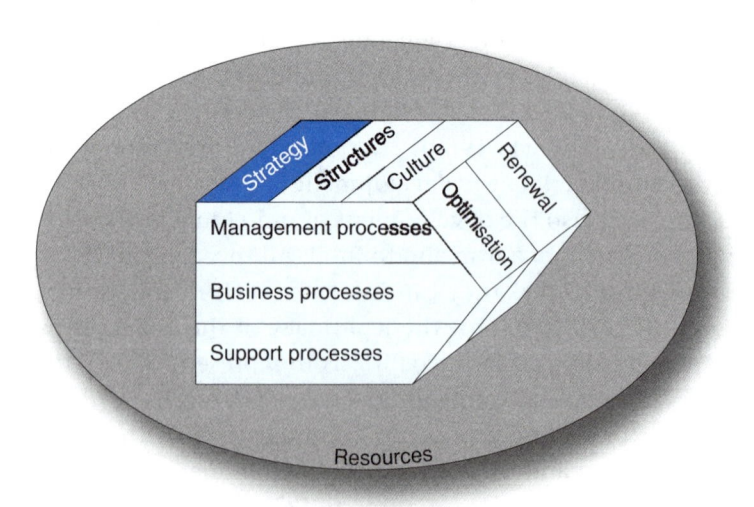

Figure 6.2 Strategy directs the activities of a firm

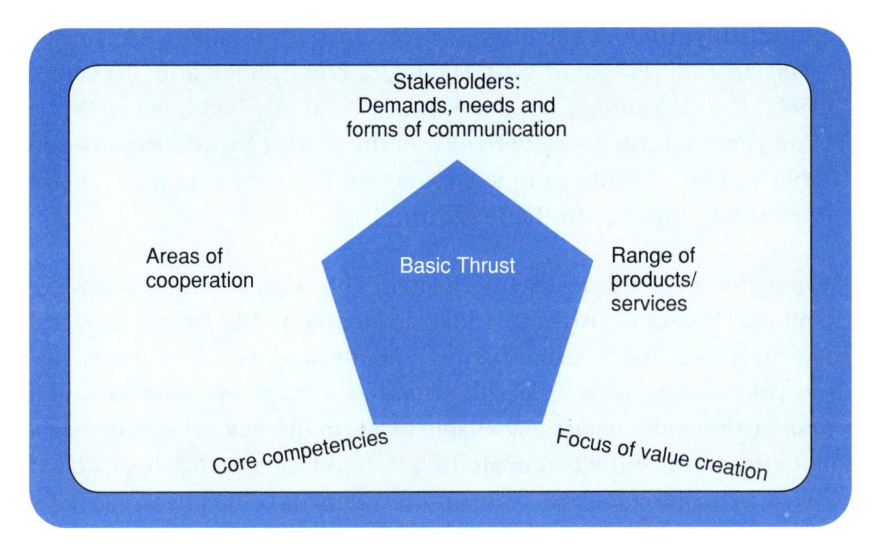

Figure 6.3 Content issues of a strategy

- First, a firm should clearly identify the *relevant stakeholders*, their *needs* and their *demands* that the firm aims to satisfy. On the one hand, this means identifying target groups and target markets, both on the *supplier and customer* sides, but also relevant target (customer) segments and their expectations on the *labour market* and *capital market*. On the other hand, a firm should develop methods of communication in order to establish and maintain optimum contact with stakeholders.
- Secondly, a firm should define its *range of offerings* (products and services) as well as the benefits to be created for each target group. This also raises fundamental questions about achieving the desired price segment.
- Thirdly, when establishing the *focus of value creation*, firms should clarify the particular part in their total value creation process (in terms of the optimal depth of production[24]) on which they concentrate or to which they wish to restrict themselves. In other words, which parts of the entire value creation chain (Porter, 1985) does a firm want to cover and which parts of the work does it want to leave (e.g. outsource) to others.
- This impacts on the definition of the *areas of cooperation*, for choosing with *whom to cooperate with*, and for the structure of *cooperation* with these particular partners.

- And fifthly, there is the question concerning the *capabilities* or *core competencies* (Prahalad and Hamel, 1990; Hamel and Prahalad, 1994) that are already apparent or must initially be forged so that a firm can establish a strong brand on the market by offering sustainable and also ideally unique benefits for its customers that remain constantly superior in the long run.

These five areas are closely interrelated. This means that they must be examined simultaneously rather than sequentially. The conclusions and goals drawn up by this examination embody *strategic orientation knowledge*. This knowledge is especially useful as a frame of reference when *allocating the limited resources* available to a firm (money, labour, management attention), and when exploiting or rejecting *opportunities* (such as options to acquire another company or offers of cooperation made by other companies).

The act of examining these five areas and, thereby, establishing corresponding goals leads to the *configuration* of a firm's desired future *strategic position* (Pümpin, 1992), which should enable a firm to gain a *long-term competitive advantage* compared to its competitors. It should be stressed that *configuration* signifies a strategic position evolving out of *coherent interplay* between the most varied of goals and capabilities.

It might be prudent to cluster business activities when there is a wide *variation* in the range of work, in the corresponding value creation activities, or in the buyer's needs. In this case, a *business segmentation*[25] is carried out (cf. Abell, 1980, pp. 169ff; Ansoff, 1984, pp. 37ff), and subsequently a so-called *business strategy* is developed for each business unit which specifies the range of customer needs, offerings and capabilities of each business unit. On a firm level, these business (unit) strategies need to be integrated into a *corporate strategy* (cf. Gomez, 1999, pp. 31ff).

Strategic goals, which do not describe the necessary resources or their mobilisation or how to achieve the goals, remain noble but vague declarations of intent. This, in addition to the strategy *content*, introduces the second important aspect of a strategy, namely, the careful design of a *strategy process* that increases the probability of success. A workable strategy may by no means be limited to mere statements detailing the firm's goals; rather, it must also demonstrate *concrete ways of developing and realising* adequate goals.

In particular, every strategy should be *made actionable* by using a portfolio of strategic initiatives (or projects). For every *strategic initiative*, all the goals, vital resources, important interdependencies between the individual projects, relevant stakeholders and specific expectations of and towards these stakeholders, a procedural plan and schedule as well as the cornerstones of a workable project structure must be clarified and agreed upon in a binding manner and then continuously refined during the realisation of the intended strategy.

6.3.2 Perspectives on strategy development

Theories about strategy development are among the most controversial areas of research in management studies. Mintzberg (1998) outlines ten different schools of thought and thereby offers an introduction to this subject. However, a single, prescriptive approach will be introduced here, the approach by the so-called Design School (cf. Fig. 9).

Fig. 9 does not only depict an ideal typical procedure, but it also portrays two theoretical approaches (perspectives) concerning what we may expect of a successful strategy: on the left hand side is the outside-in perspective, on the right hand side the inside-out perspective.

6.3.2.1 Outside-in perspective

The *outside-in perspective*, the so-called *market-based view*, emphasises the fundamental necessity of systematically examining a firm's environment and, in particular, its *industry*. In terms of the degree of competition and the corresponding attractiveness of the market, the development of a strategy needs to address how to position the firm (or its individual business units) within its external environment (market, competition, industry) in order to achieve *sustainable competitive advantage*. From this perspective, the *starting point* for the development of a strategy includes the opportunities, threats and risks in the environment, i.e. the structure of a particular industry. To illustrate this, we can imagine a firm that strives to become the market leader with one of its products: the starting point of the analysis is the commercial market in which the firm sells its product. Based on an analysis of other suppliers in this market – in other words the competitors – and of environmental opportunities and threats, the firm decides to aim for market leadership. To achieve this goal, decisions are subsequently taken and measures implemented that affect the 'core' of the firm, for example, expanding the sales network in order to increase turnover.

According to the outside-in perspective, the strategic success of a firm hinges upon identifying a market with a high attractiveness (in terms

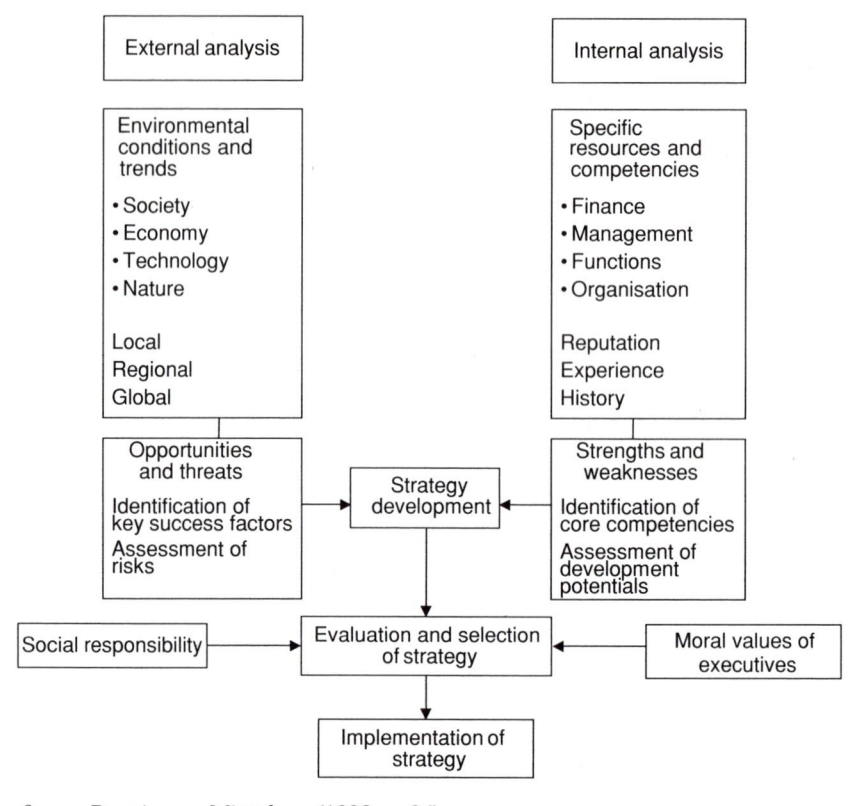

```
                    ┌──────────────────┐                    ┌──────────────────┐
                    │ External analysis│                    │ Internal analysis│
                    └──────────────────┘                    └──────────────────┘

        ┌─────────────────────────┐               ┌─────────────────────────┐
        │ Environmental           │               │ Specific                │
        │ conditions and          │               │ resources and           │
        │ trends                  │               │ competencies            │
        │                         │               │                         │
        │ • Society               │               │ • Finance               │
        │ • Economy               │               │ • Management            │
        │ • Technology            │               │ • Functions             │
        │ • Nature                │               │ • Organisation          │
        │                         │               │                         │
        │ Local                   │               │ Reputation              │
        │ Regional                │               │ Experience              │
        │ Global                  │               │ History                 │
        └─────────────────────────┘               └─────────────────────────┘
```

Figure 6.4 Development of a strategy according to the so-called Design School

(External branch): Opportunities and threats / Identification of key success factors / Assessment of risks → Strategy development

(Internal branch): Strengths and weaknesses / Identification of core competencies / Assessment of development potentials → Strategy development

Social responsibility → Evaluation and selection of strategy ← Moral values of executives

↓ Implementation of strategy

Source: Drawing on Mintzberg (1998, p. 26).

of growth and profit expectations) and then drawing up a competitive strategy (e.g. a niche strategy, cost leadership), which offers the greatest chances of success. The most decisive factors are the search for an attractive industry, an appropriate definition of the firm's own business units (Abell, 1980; Ansoff, 1984) and the establishment of suitable competitive strategies (Porter, 1980, 1985).[26]

6.3.2.2 Inside-out perspective

The *inside-out perspective*, the so-called *resource-based view*, takes up the argument from the opposite point of view. Organically evolved *capabilities* and *resources* of a firm form the starting point of analysis.[27] By harnessing mostly unique capabilities and resources, a firm itself can influence the rules of the competitive game to create an advantageous environment (market dynamics) for itself (Hamel and Prahalad, 1994). Since the beginning of the nineties, firms have shown a growing interest in this perspective. Before this, the competitive environment with its opportunities and risks played the key role. According to this perspective then a firm will achieve sustainable competitive advantage whenever it succeeds in mobilising *resources* and developing *capabilities* (*competencies*) that are *valuable, rare, inimitable* (or almost inimitable) and *non-substitutable* (Barney, 1991, pp. 101ff) and that enable a firm to shape the environment to its own advantage.

6.3.3 Resources and core competencies

Resources are tradable material and immaterial commodities (goods and rights) needed to carry out value added activities effectively and efficiently. Among material resources are, for example, buildings, machinery, and information technology. Know-how is the key immaterial resource and includes commercial patents, licences, copyrights and even to a certain degree the non-tradable knowledge of the workforce. Specific *competencies* in a firm are required in order to acquire, mobilise, combine, and develop resources. These competencies comprise both a more *cognitive* aspect, namely *knowledge*, and *practical abilities*, i.e. *intelligent processes* and *organisational routines*. The structure of these processes and routines (process patterns) mirror the organisational knowledge and contribute to the optimal use of available resources (Nelson and Winter, 1982).

Thus, the inside-out perspective emphasises above all the need for a *systematic development of competencies* as a key task of strategic management. Success or failure is determined by whether a firm can cultivate rare, not easily imitable and non-substitutable *core competencies* that help to achieve, both the firm and its customers, long-term competitive advantage. Core competencies are, therefore, the unique capabilities of a firm, which in comparison to all competitors, offer the customer a superior product and service and by so doing create sustainable competitive advantage (Bogner and Thomas, 1994).

Core competencies are normally characterised by the fact that they are applicable to *several business units* at once, thus offering firms the possibility to expand upon them, i.e. utilising them with different products and methods of production (Prahalad and Hamel, 1990).

At most, firms can normally boast one or two core competencies. These are based on *unique knowledge* and *superbly practised organisational routines*. The decisive significance of *knowledge* in developing and realising a successful strategy has led to the emergence of *knowledge management* in recent years (e.g. von Krogh and Venzin, 1995).

In addition, a second important trend can be identified in strategy theory. As markets grow together under the umbrella of globalisation, there is increasing division of labour and specialisation. Firms conceive themselves more and more obliged to concentrate firmly on those activities in the value creation chain (Porter, 1985) in which they can take full advantage of their core competencies. Everything else will be handled by *outsourcing* to suppliers who are, if possible, just as capable as they are reliable, or it will be achieved in close cooperation with selected partners. A company's depth of production is thus reduced, which explains why the average firm size tends to be more in decline than expansion, despite the many growth strategies that are oftentimes observed.

When the partners with whom a firm cooperates are also competitors, there is a blend of cooperation and competition, '*coopetition*', with corresponding opportunities and risks. An example of this is the joint development and production of a large-sized limousine by rivals Volkswagen and Ford. The van is marketed by both automotive companies under their own brand name. Such strategic decisions can be supported considerably through the use of *game theory* (Nalebuff and Brandenburger, 1996).

6.4 Structures of a firm

6.4.1 Differentiation and integration

The emergence of complex organisations is to be understood largely against the background of the rise of ever *larger* (and more efficient) markets and the development towards a *growing division of labour* in our society.[28] The *sinking transaction costs* for transporting physical goods (invention of the railway, cars and aeroplanes) and for the transmission of data (invention of the telephone, radio, television, computer and the Internet) have set the stage for a huge expansion of markets in the last two centuries and have ultimately led to today's world economy of labour division and globalisation of markets. This development is indicative of the experience that *differentiation*, i.e., the division of labour and specialisation, has particular *efficiency advantages*, whether in the field of industrial assembly or in administration. When talking about efficiency advantages, we mean the phenomenon that more output can be achieved with lower costs and in less time through

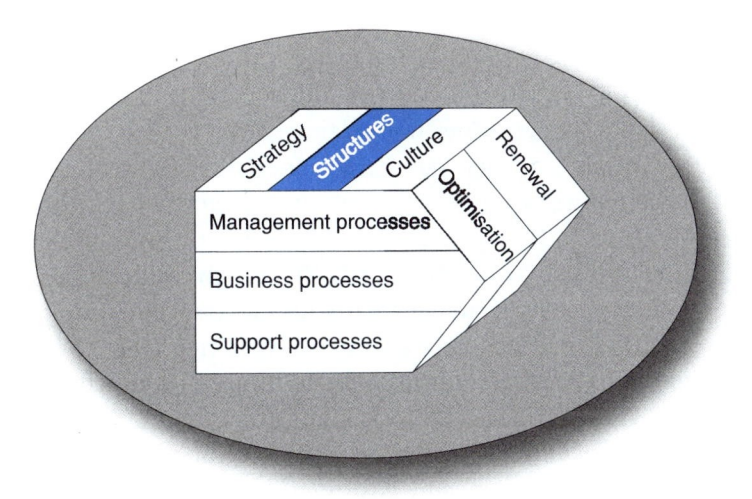

Figure 6.5   Structures coordinate behaviour

a skilful *division of labour* (and labour organisations), a suitable *qualification* of the workforce and, to some extent, a *standardisation* of both processes and products or services.

Intermediate outputs produced under a division of labour must be integrated in a precise manner during the course of a production process. Therefore, organisations which operate in this way require suitable *coordinating mechanisms* for the *integration* of completed individual work into a meaningful whole. The advantages of efficiency from the division of labour and standardisation are thus juxtaposed against the costs of coordination.

In the past, the guarantee of equal rights was sufficient to force public bureaucracies towards greater standardisation and efficiency. However, *division of labour, specialisation,* and *standardisation* in the industrial field, all spawned by the dawn of mass production, quickly allowed a large proportion of the population to afford such modern technological innovations as their own private car.

More than 200 years since the beginning of the industrial revolution, however, the division of labour, specialisation and standardisation continue to remain key challenges of a firm's business activity. In today's world, it is not only industrial production processes (car, computer, foodstuffs) that are standardised, but increasingly also how new products are developed (processes of product innovation) or how services are provided, whether those services are in a financial or even a medical field ('the industrialisation of services'). Standardisation, however, does not mean that the variety of products is reduced. On the contrary: the variety is increasing dramatically. Firms must increasingly concentrate on guaranteeing their customers the greatest benefit. They can do this by working towards so-called integrated business solutions (Belz, 1997) through a *customer-specific integration* of standardised intermediate outputs (mainly more or less complex modules) that generate a superior customer value. A considerable amount of modern innovations is, therefore, based upon a clever game of standardisation of which customers are unaware, and upon customer-specific combination and integration, which really constitute the core of the specific customer value.

Structures enable to:

- define a suitable *division of labour* (differentiation) and thus allow gains in efficiency and productivity, on the one hand; and
- *coordinate* intermediate outputs created in a division of labour, on the other hand, so that they can be *integrated* effectively into a greater whole.

Differentiation, therefore, helps primarily in establishing the most cost-effective production processes with the aim of *efficiency*: 'the maximum possible output with the minimum possible input'. *Integration* helps primarily in generating the greatest possible benefit to customers with the aim of *effectiveness*: 'to be as precise as possible in meeting those quality requirements of a service previously agreed upon with the stakeholders'.

Structures maintain everything that shows a certain degree of *temporal constancy*. In this sense, a structure is an expression of *order* or *organisation* (Probst, 1987). In terms of business management, we can differentiate between two important categories of structure: *organisational* and *process* structures.

6.4.2 Organisational structure

In the division of labour, be they immediate value-added activities or leadership tasks, a company's organisational structure reveals the *fun-*

damental criteria that dictate how its tasks and activities are *grouped together* and then *carried out*. For example according to:

- *functions* (e.g. research and development, purchasing, production, marketing, human resources, finance, etc.). Here we can talk of a *functional organisation*.
- *market- or product-related areas of activity* (e.g. pharma specialities, generics, OTC products, nutrition, eye care, animal health). Here we can talk of a *divisional organisation.*
- *geographical areas* or *regions* (e.g. Switzerland, Germany, France, Italy or Europe, USA, Latin America, Africa, Asia). Here we can talk of a *country organisation* or a *regional organisation*.

In reality, however, a variety of combinations exist. For instance, a divisional unit within a multidivisional company can be structured aligned to

Executive Committee					
Marketing / Sales	Logistics	Research and Development		Production	Financial controlling Administration
Sales Manager	Planning	Statics		Manufacturing of Components	Controlling
Product Manager	Make or Buy	Construction		Surface Treatment	Finance
Customer Support	Stock Control	System Integration		Cell Construction	Human Resources
Advertising / Public Relations		Certification		Assembly	Accounting
Marketing Support		Methodology		Aircraft Maintenance	Information Technology Organisational Development
				Subsidiary Operations	

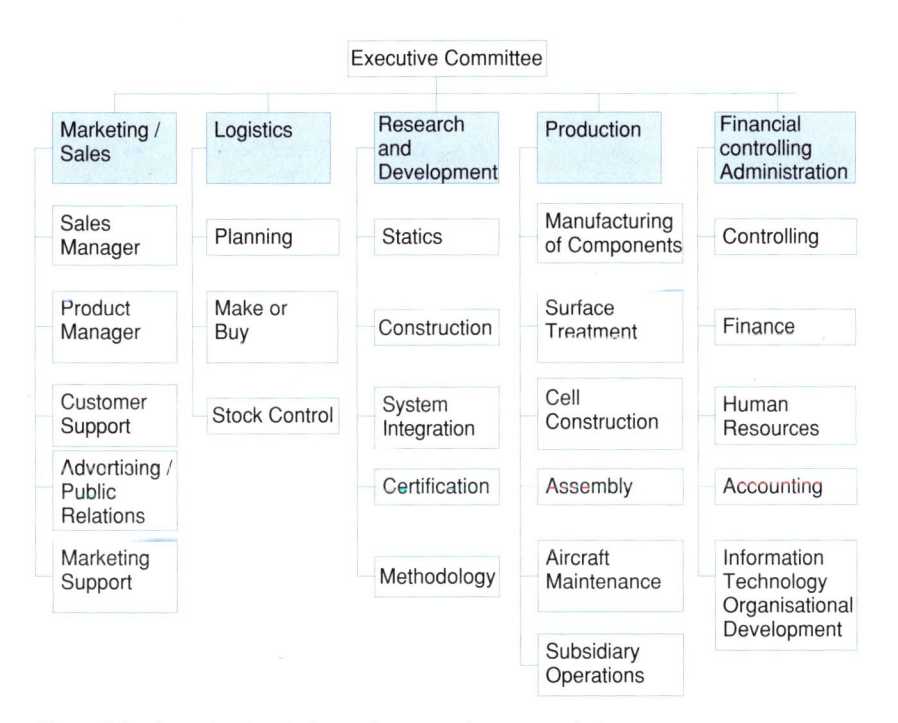

Figure 6.6 Organisational chart of an aeroplane manufacturer

functions. Or a group company (country organisation) can itself be structured according to divisions.

Organisational structures can be graphically illustrated by using an organisational chart (cf. for example, Fig. 11), which depicts the aggregation of tasks to major departments, but also the formal power relations and communication channels (chain of command) between different departments and the executives at the top of the company.

6.4.3 Process structures

Process structures determine *which tasks* and in which *sequential order* they have to be accomplished. Process structures thus primarily facilitate skilful *time coordination*, i.e. a *synchronisation* of work tasks or work task areas (cf. Fig. 12).

In recent years, an examination of procedures and processes has gained dramatically in significance. What is important now is not only doing the *right* thing and doing it *right*, but also doing it at the *right time*. Customers increasingly want to be satisfied as quickly as possible and as closely as possible to the agreed time. In today's market, the

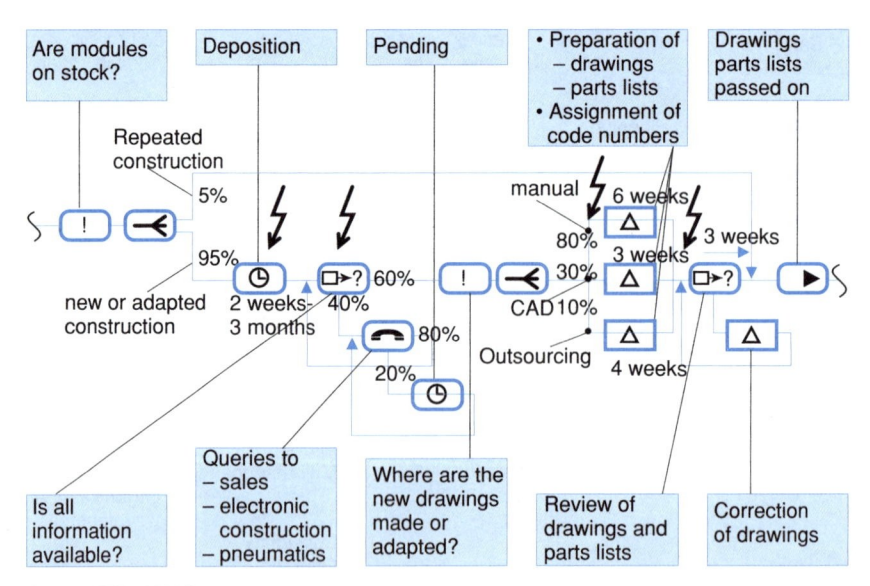

Source: ITEM-HSG.
Figure 6.7 Example of a process map

claims of service quality, therefore, not only include a service's objective makeup, but also its *speed*, *punctuality* and *reliability*. This development has not least been augmented through the opportunities offered by modern information and communication technologies. On the one hand, these opportunities afford businesses new tools to coordinate their work, and on the other hand, they forcibly change the dynamics of competition towards a *contest of time and speed* ('time to market', 'time to money').

Process structures enable to ensure that procedures follow similar *patterns*, having a certain degree of *standardisation* linked to time savings, amongst other things. Forming and developing suitable process structures nowadays falls under the scope of *process management*, which we will examine in detail in section 7.4.

6.4.4 Structural regulations

Organisational and process structures are revealed in a variety of structural (or organisational) regulations. These regulations should establish *order* and usually result from *authorised decisions*. Among these are as already mentioned, organisational charts, job descriptions with accountability and responsibility of specific positions, flow charts, rules, directives, and all sorts of handbooks (organisational handbook, quality handbook). Additionally, there are local arrangements (determination of site location), spatial arrangements (layout of production equipment, positioning of work stations) and arrangements for information technology.

These regulations result in certain forms of *division of labour*, of *coordination*, and of *leadership*. They also engender specific *relationships* among a firm's people and among its departments. Finally, the regulations result in the types of *organisational structure* and *process structures* that were discussed above and that together determine the logical and sequential structure of a firm's activities and processes.

6.4.5 The Processes of *structuration*

Structures are, therefore, generated – just like strategies – not simply of their own accord, rather they need to be designed based on specific objectives. A firm's endeavour to optimise and renew requires it to monitor and develop its structures continuously. New regulations and practices alter structures (and thus the organisation or 'order' of a firm) in order to meet specific business goals more effectively.

This does not, however, mean that a firm can be assembled and developed on the drawing board as if it were a technical machine. Firms are complex formations based on the division of labour, in which people from a range of cultural, occupational, and private contexts work together. They are characterised by particular origins, particular experiences and perspectives, feelings, personal interests and their own individual, unique views on life.

The available options of individuals to freely behave in everyday life and the closely associated, unpredictable interaction dynamics among persons, departments and their tasks strictly bound each idea of technocratic feasibility in organisational settings. In other words, it would be an extremely reductionist (trivial) idea to assume that the organisational elite at the top of a firm could control every event within the firm in detail by autocratically implementing sophisticated structural regulations and control mechanisms, even if such decisions can create extreme effects, both expected and unexpected.

The emergence of structures, whether they be the organisational structure or process structures (as the result of systematic process development), is *in itself an enactment process*. Structures and routines arise over the course of time through an interplay of events, human contributions and appropriate or less appropriate interventions (Wilke, 1996b). Much initiative and detailed work is required from the most varied of people in a firm until, for instance, an order fulfilment process with short lead times or a smooth research and development process has become fully internalised. Order or organisation thus ensues from the *processes of structuration* (Giddens, 1984), involving a host of people in a variety of ways and in differing degrees.

Therefore, *processes of structuration* and the *structures thus enacted* stand in an iterative, circular and recursive relationship with one another. This is because, once developed, structures will always define the scope of development, i.e. the structural conditions and context, for any ensuing structuration processes.

Therefore, all activities associated with managing or organising a firm, in general, take place within an established structural (and cultural) *context* that enables a firm to perceive (and practice) many activities as useful, reasonable and even imperative, while highlighting others as inappropriate and useless. It is, therefore, not only people who organise a firm, additionally, there will also always be other factors 'involved' in enacting

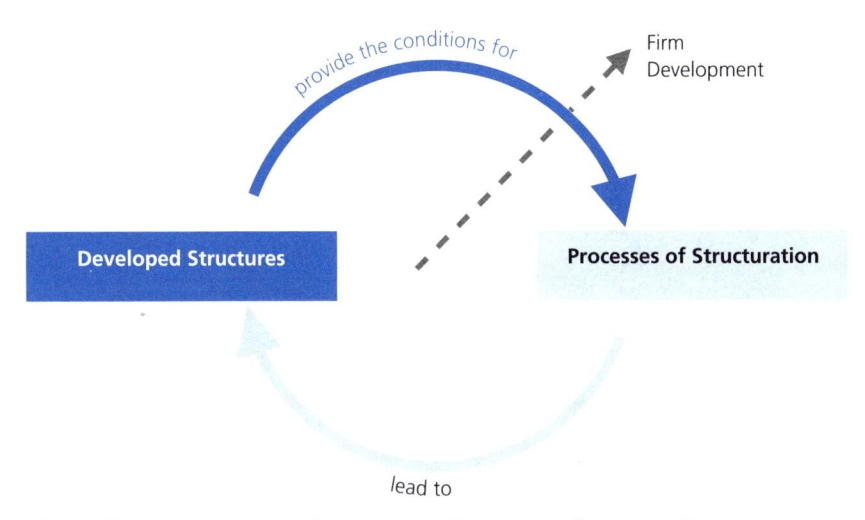

Figure 6.8 Iterative nature of structures and processes of structuration

order, such as the established structures and the continuous processes of communication and interaction. In this respect, firms can be understood as self-organising (or self-referential) systems.[29]

Structures are often perceived to be restrictive or even repressive. Such an understanding fails to recognise that structures inhibit both limiting as well as enabling forces. Thus, the choice of a certain type of word processing software limits all employees in the firm to a very specific program. In contrast, however, the same structural regulation also has an 'enabling' effect, since this very harmonisation of word processing software applications allow the entire workforce to easily exchange and develop documents collectively. The same applies to the choice of a certain company language, such as English or Spanish.

6.5 The culture of a firm

6.5.1 Elements of a culture

Explicit structural arrangements and regulations are not by themselves sufficient for enabling a firm to cope with the many needs, demands and stimuli both within and outside of its immediate environment within a satisfactory timeframe. In addition, a *shared sense of purpose*, a

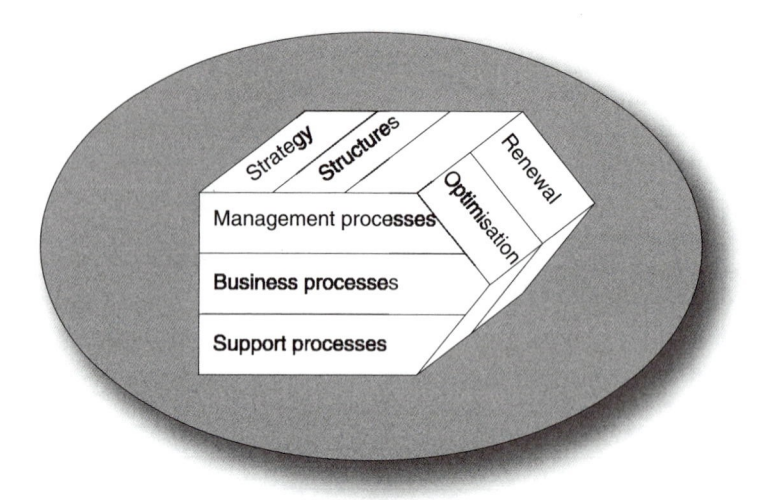

Figure 6.9 A culture creates meaning and identity

common explicit or implicit *background knowledge*, is required; it enables businesses new ways of:

- understanding and applying regulations and guidelines appropriately;
- placing unpredictable, uncertain and ambiguous events and developments in a meaningful general context and, then, using this foundation to remain collectively viable and able to take action.

What does this shared sense of purpose comprise? There are two forces, referred here as 'shaping forces'. They either have a material manifestation, such as artworks or artefacts with significant symbolic effect (e.g. flags, large scale logos, architectural design elements), or they are of an immaterial nature.

Immaterial shaping forces might include shared, yet unwritten *expectations*, *common experiences* composed in stories or even myths and the related *attitudes, unwritten rules* and *implicit contracts*[30] that help to *create order* and contribute to the enactment of *taken-for-granted routines.*[31]

In their entirety, these immaterial shaping forces – and also in part the shaping forces which have been materially embodied through symbols – form the *culture* of a firm, meaning that they create a natural sense of purpose that provides a degree of orientation.

The term *culture* embraces, in essence, all *symbolic references* and *certainties* around which we all naturally orient ourselves in our day-to-day words and deeds and upon which we can rely. The central elements of a corporate culture are, for example:

- basic assumptions;
- attitudes;
- norms and values;
- identity in general, departmental identities and their interplay;
- stories and myths about important changes, important choices or critical incidents in the company's history;
- patterns of discourse (typical argumentation chains and patterns of interpretation);
- company language (use of abbreviations, special notions, etc.);
- collective expectations and inherent beliefs.

People use these symbolic references in everyday thoughts and actions, largely subconsciously, and by the very action of using them guarantee their continuous reproduction.[32]

In this sense, a corporate culture can be compared with the shaping forces (or structuring forces) of a language, e.g. with grammar and semantics:

- On the one hand, reasonable linguistic understanding will always be reliant on grammatical rules and semantic agreements – albeit without us needing to be aware of it. A four-year-old child can make himself or herself understood through the use of language, but without ever having studied grammar or semantics.
- On the other hand, shaping forces in the form of rules and agreements reveal their effect only when 'used', i.e. through the use of language. It is precisely through this means that the shaping forces are enacted, updated and recreated.

A corporate culture is, therefore, comparable with the grammatical rules and semantic agreements in a language, or with a *linguistic community*.

6.5.2 Differentiation of culture

There is frequent talk of 'the' culture of a firm, as if it were some homogenous monolith. This is not unproblematic because some specialised working teams in a firm need to interrelate frequently with external parties. This leads, for example, to the problem that communities-of-practice (Brown and Duguid, 1991; Wenger, 1998) in direct contact with the market – compared to their colleagues in logistics, production or in research and development – might develop their own entirely different assumptions and very distinct perceptions concerning the strategic success factors for the firm's business activity or the quality of good work.

We can often observe major cultural differences between individual value-added processes within a firm. In the areas of research and development, for example, a playful exuberance for technology and its use in new products often exists. In the production function, by contrast, discipline, punctuality and security play a much greater role. Thus, while scientific expertise, creativity, a spirit of discovery and inspiration matter in the area of *innovation*; it is reliability, precision, security, and punctuality that are important for *order fulfilment*. In line with these differences, there are often two distinct structural arrangements: in the area of innovation, there are open work spaces and few guidelines, in production, there are clear procedural guidelines and a comparably rigid code of behaviour. How can such different working spheres with such distinct structures and cultures emerge?

Everyday occurrences are constantly being observed in businesses, i.e. there are ongoing processes of *perception* and *interpretation*. We can, therefore, talk of *'concurrent observation'*.[33] Through concurrent observation, people in firms select certain events from a continuous stream of events, and then enact their own connections between them, ultimately drawing *meaningful descriptions* or *accounts* from them. These descriptions *never* constitute 'the one' reality, but they have a character that can create a sense of purpose for individuals, but can also serve to explain,[34] legitimise[35] or instruct.[36]

Observation, therefore, does not in any way limit itself to an inner-psychological scrutiny of events in the minds of the individual observers. On the contrary, it is conducted primarily in the *everyday communicative and relational processes*. People select other people with whom they have a *trusting relationship* whenever something happens, something significant or ambiguous and potentially also having unpredictable consequences – thus in need of careful interpretation and explanation. This could include the merger of two tough competitors, the bankruptcy of an important supplier, the merger of two departments of the own firm, the questionable behaviour of a good colleague, etc. People are interested in what others think about the same event. In a complex *collective process of discursive interpretation,* from the perspective of their *local context,* particularly meaningful descriptions (interpretations) are negotiated. Over time, these privileged interpretations will gradually achieve to have unquestionable validity and legitimacy, despite being descriptions of descriptions of descriptions of descriptions.

Through *communicative* processes, people will have to agree upon the *appropriateness of certain descriptions* for each new event. This means that the appropriateness and validity of descriptions must to some extent, be *negotiated* in discussions (cf. in detail also Sandner and Meyer, 1994). Descriptions are discursive *'constructions'* of system members. Thus what is known about 'the' social reality as such develops from a *collective process of construction and confirmation* (Berger and Luckmann, 1966). This is especially true of strategic orientation knowledge.

Looking at it from a different angle, a *differentiation of culture* arises from different *discursive examinations,* i.e. from the *collective interpretations* as people master the challenges they encounter in their immediate everyday work. This differentiation of culture also finds expression in different structures. Variations in any organically evolved corporate culture and in its structures thus arise from the fact that a firm's value creation processes require people to work on *diverse tasks.* These people and the corresponding communities-of-practice are linked inwardly and outwardly in *different networks of interactions* with *differing frequencies of contact* with one another.

Through such routinised discourses a series of 'standard descriptions' and 'standard explanations' become established in every business during the course of time. They concern questions that repeatedly demand meaningful answers. These questions might concern the own *identity* (who are we? what are our goals? what is our 'mission'?); or *suitable working conditions, division of labour* and *leadership* (what is our role as executives? what 'is' success of our firm?); they might concern the *treatment of customers* (what is important in the way we deal with customers?); or *how certain problems are handled* (if we must choose, which is more important: time or perfection?).

These 'standard descriptions' or world views can assume *different 'local' forms* depending on area, department or team. In other words, they can assume the character of a *local theory,*[37] and the differences between the local theories of different functions or professions can become constructive or destructive sources of friction or even lasting conflict, especially along the points of contact (interfaces).

Visible, materialised conditions (structures) are the result of the organisational members' past actions. In that sense, they reflect their (immaterial) local theories and can be reinforced by the materialised structures. As structures gradually materialise, they instantly act as both enabling and restricting conditions. More specifically, people create their own (or other people's) work environments according to the ideas of a local theory. This local theory emerges from the collective (discursive) interpretations of everyday occurrences and continues to recreate itself through these very interpretations. As people go about their everyday business activity, they collect experiences in the context of materialised (visible) conditions. These conditions have arisen from the ideas of the local theory and their materialisation then works to *confirm* or *call into question* the local theory itself. There is thus a circular logic to the development of local theories, to processes of structuration and to the emergence of materialised structures and everyday routines. In other words, they are self-organising or self-referential[38] (cf. fig. 15).

This difficult theoretical description demonstrates clearly that it is simpler to change specific structures than it is to influence a culture. While company executives can alter the structures of a firm comparatively quickly in any processes of change, in the sense of a classical restructuring, much greater effort is needed to steer the barely accessible cultural elements of an organisation, including local theories and organisational routines, in a new direction. The following representation of the organisational iceberg illustrates this graphically (cf. Fig. 16).

6.6 Routinisation through structuring forces

What is the *lasting legacy* of effective structuring forces, such as strategy, structures or corporate culture? We could say that the legacy manifests itself in 'frozen decisions'. Over time, the processes of developing strategy, structures and culture generate all that should remain *more or less constant and stable*. A more efficient use of limited resources, which certainly includes time as well, requires that firms *should not have to start from scratch, re-inventing and re-negotiating* the successful fulfilment of a complex order or carrying out a difficult R&D project. Rather, the people involved should be able to rely on certain structuring forces.

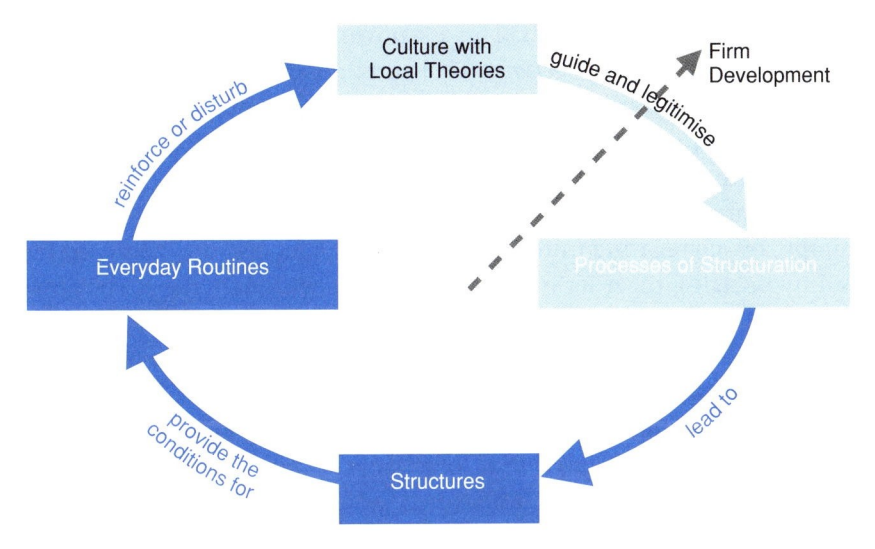

Figure 6.10 Circular logic of local theories and structure development

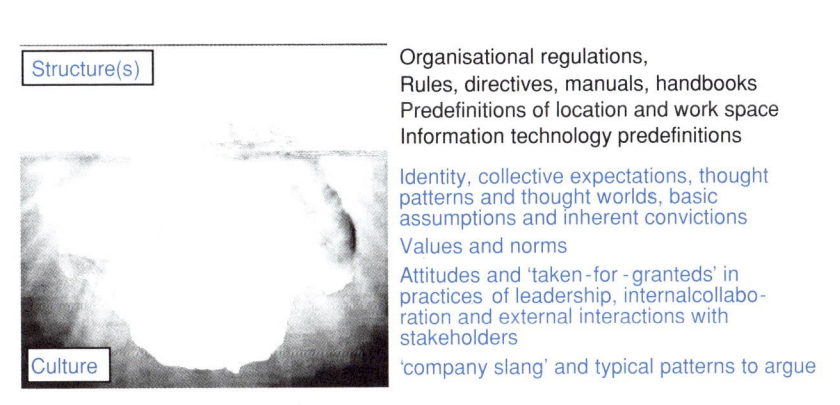

Structure(s)	Organisational regulations, Rules, directives, manuals, handbooks Predefinitions of location and work space Information technology predefinitions
Culture	Identity, collective expectations, thought patterns and thought worlds, basic assumptions and inherent convictions Values and norms Attitudes and 'taken-for-granteds' in practices of leadership, internal collaboration and external interactions with stakeholders 'company slang' and typical patterns to argue

Source: Drawing on French and Bell, 1973.
Figure 6.11 The organisational iceberg

These structuring forces include not only all types of plans, principles, rules, regulations, and handbooks, but also commonly shared experiences and unwritten rules – perhaps composed in stories or even myths – which in their interactions constitute a form of expectations horizon, or an interwoven expectations structure (cf. in more detail also section 6.5).

Over time, certain typical patterns of communication and practice may emerge when firms repeatedly and successfully accomplish similar tasks and challenges. This is known as the *routinisation* *of the organisational stream of actions*. To a certain extent, the development of structuring forces, such as strategy, structures, and culture, and the routinisation of the organisational stream of actions represent two sides of the same coin.[39]

The routinisation of organisational practices certainly does not arise simply by aggregating unrelated individual practices. It is achieved by subtly bringing together individual practices with daily work cooperation that embraces people, departments and even firms. The latter implies that as a firm's strategy, structures and culture develop, then, not only do its employees gradually adopt routine behaviour but also its customers, suppliers and partners, as long as they interact with the firm. In short, it can be asserted that, over time, a thoroughly complicated and more or less carefully fine-tuned system of routines emerges in organisational communication and action.

Success is determined by, and thus reinforces, the suitability of established routines and structuring forces. Disturbance arises, however, when there is (systematic) failure, e.g. continued conflict or problems of quality. In this case, there must follow a fresh examination of, discussion about and negotiation over the structuring forces and a recalibration of the everyday routines. Thus, *routinisation* always concerns organisational and personal *qualification* in the sense of collectively developing and training new habits and routines.

However, what people actually do in routines increasingly slips from their consciousness into their subconscious mind and, over time, becomes a natural everyday act. For example, there are two phenomena that set the experienced car driver apart from a beginner:

- First of all, experienced car drivers *do not need to pay special attention* to the *mechanical* processes such as steering, signalling, shifting gears, clutch control or braking, while these demand the beginner's full concentration.
- Secondly, experienced car drivers have internalised where their *attention* (perception) should be directed, whereas the beginner is under extreme pressure contemplating a multitude of current visual inputs and previous relevant learnings at every moment (position of the car on the road, right of way, distance to the vehicle in front, etc.).

Routinisation is thus, on the one hand, evident in *habitualised mechanical control*, i.e. in certain *behavioural habits* and, on the other hand, in a *habitualised direction of attention*, i.e. in certain *habits of perceiving* and *interpreting* everyday phenomena.[40] This also applies for the work people do in a firm.[41]

Routinisation has different advantages and disadvantages.[42] An important advantage is in *speeding up processes*, which can lead to cost advantages. A second advantage is the *error reduction* caused by constantly perfecting the routines and thus leading to *quality gains*. A third advantage lies in *concentrating the focus* on the really crucial challenges with a high degree of novelty.

However, routinisation also has disadvantages. First, anything that adopts increasingly the nature of a routine gradually vanishes from our consciousness and, under certain circumstances, can disappear entirely – 'blind spot' can threaten our existence or that of our firm. Familiar perceptions and interpretations can easily lead to the unquestioned adoption of world views and fundamental beliefs.[43] Secondly, a firm must ensure that the many individual habits of its employees are carefully coordinated with one another. Changing one person's routine can lead to the necessity of 're-calibrating' the routines of many other people. Established routines that have stood the test of time thus demonstrate a strong inertia or resistance to change and a hostility towards any attempts at renewal. This has less to do with the unwillingness and reluctance of individuals to change, rather, with the *inherent durability and persistence of intricately linked interactive routines*.

The *blind spots* of a firm are formed partially by structuring forces which have developed collectively and have become accepted as normal, together with the fundamental beliefs which accompany them. In addition, blind spots are formed by habitual and customary modes of perception, interpretation and cooperation. Only those firms which are extremely receptive towards new ideas, which embrace unfamiliar ways of looking at things in the sense of linguistic images and metaphors, and that manage diversity with savvy can guard against the dangers of such blind spots.[44]

7
The *Processes* of a Firm

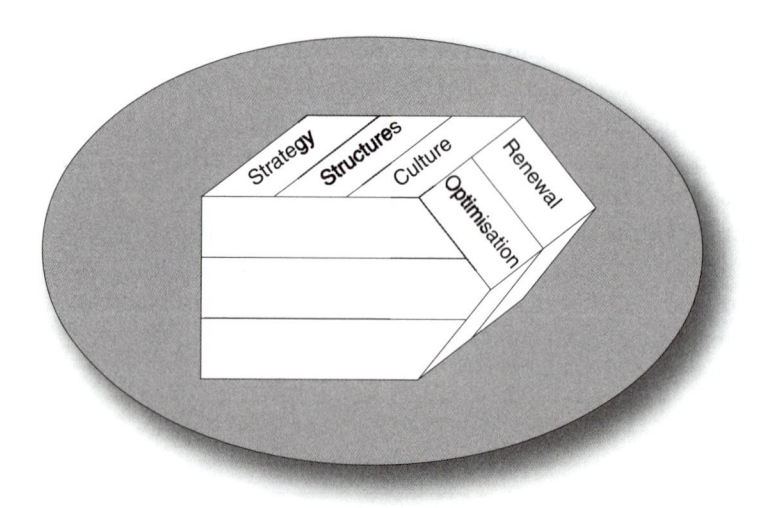

Figure 7.1   The firm as a system of processes

7.1 The process perspective

Over the last decade, changes in a firm's different environmental spheres have led to a massively increasing significance of *process structures* and also how *processes* are designed, compared to the organisational structure, i.e. how firms are structured into organisational units (Osterloh and Frost, 1998). Growing demands from customers, the deregulation and globalisation of many markets, the increasing role of the capital market, but above all, the rapid development of information and communication technologies have generated a fundamental intensification of competition. This has caused the time factor to become a competitively decisive criterion alongside quality and price. Competition, in general, is now characterised far more as a *time-based competition* than before (Stalk and Hout, 1990, 1992). We can observe that smaller fishes are not always 'swallowed up' by bigger fishes, but also that *slower* fishes are swallowed up by *quicker* ones.

In order to be able to survive in this time-based competition, the company's processes must be slimmed down as far as possible and directed towards reinforcing the firm's own core competencies. This must be done by *minimising the error prone interfaces* and, in the sense of 'lean management' (Imai, 1989; Womack, et al. 1990), by systematically *eliminating all 'blind work'* (non value-added work) that generates no customer benefit. An important starting point to achieve this is in applying an organisation's horizontal perspective, i.e. the *value creation processes*, as the central point of reference when structuring the organisation (cf. Fig. 18).[45] A *horizontal* structure focused on customer-oriented processes thus widens the scope or even completely substitutes the traditional *vertical* structure of a firm according to *functions* (e.g. marketing, production, procurement and logistics, research and development).

Coordinating and sychronising the punctuality of task completion within departments and even the whole firm can be demonstrably supported by suitably employing applications of modern information and communication technologies.[46] The horizontal perspective has the additional advantage of facilitating a systematic perspective of the value chain that *begins and ends with the customer*. This means grouping (the process of) work logically for maximum customer benefit. For example, looking at the process of order fulfilment, we can observe that the customer stands both at the beginning of the process, e.g. at the initial contact with the sales representative, as well as at the end, e.g. at the delivery of the goods, at the customer's payment of the bill or at any after-sales support services.

7.2 Elements of a process

We consider a process as a series (or a system) of activities, which should be accomplished in a more or less standard preset sequence (activity chain), and where this accomplishment can be radically facilitated by employing information systems. The added value of a process comprises (intermediate) work outputs for internal or external process customers.

The five following elements describe a *process* in detail (cf. Österle, 1995, pp. 48ff; Müller, 1999, pp. 159ff.):

- The *activity chain* illustrates the most important tasks of a process and their correct sequence. In this chain, we can differentiate between a *macro-level* and a *micro-level*. While the macro-level offers an overview of the entire process, the micro-level provides such a high level of detail in the activity descriptions that they afford the employees clear instructions for their work.
- An *activity* is a business task which:
  - is carried out by people and/or machines;

Processes	Organisational Units (Functions)						
	Marketing	Sales	Research & Development	Procurement & Logistics	Production	Quality Management	Finance & Accounting
Market Development	Traditional design principle of organisations Specialisation based on functions and optimisation of resource deployment						
Order Processing							
Product Development					New design principle of organisations Integration through business processes and focus on customer value as well as minimisation of processing time		
Strategy Development and Controlling							

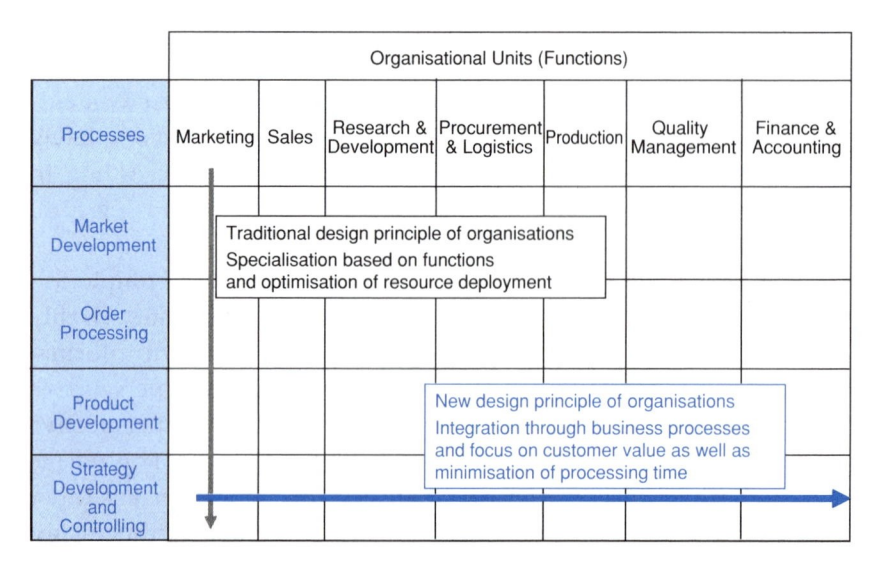

Figure 7.2 Schematic illustration of a process-oriented firm

- is dependent upon certain *inputs* (data, material) from *suppliers to the process*,
- must lead to a specific *outcome* (outputs, results), which must be delivered to internal or external *customers of the process*. The performance can be *material* (in the sense of a concrete and tangible product) or *immaterial* (in the sense of a service).
- An *information system* can support the completion of activities through applications and databases.
- *Process control* involves prioritising on-going tasks (triage function[47]), fine-tuning the on-going fulfilment of tasks in the everyday work of the firm and optimising the management of available resources. So that the quality of how processes are managed might be systematically improved, the relevant *key performance indicators* must be defined.
- *Process development* contains the basic structure and the further development of a process.

When we utilise this process perspective consequently, then we see that every firm can be understood as a *system of processes*, encompassing a variety of inter-dependent factors as well as relationships between customers and suppliers. This system of processes is often referred to as *process architecture* (Österle, 1995, pp. 61f., 137).

7.3 Process categories

Systemically mirroring the firm's value added as a *value chain* is not a novel idea.[48]

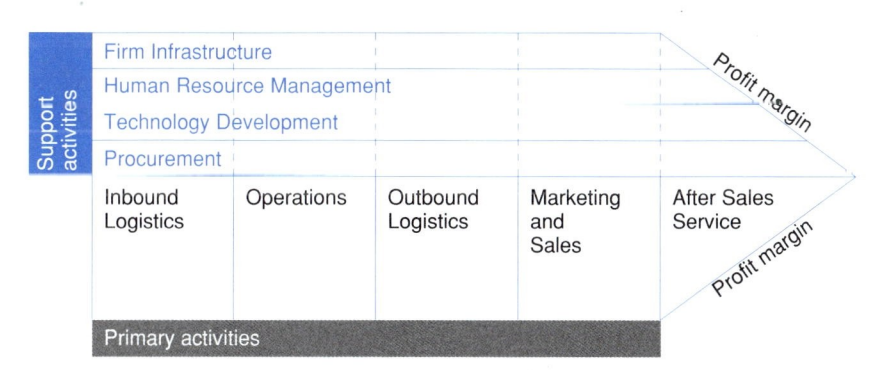

Support activities	Firm Infrastructure				
	Human Resource Management				
	Technology Development				
	Procurement				
	Inbound Logistics	Operations	Outbound Logistics	Marketing and Sales	After Sales Service
Primary activities					

Source: Porter, 1985, pp. 62, 74
Figure 7.3 Value chain

Porter (1985) differentiates between *primary activities*, which directly contribute to the customer benefit, and *supporting activities*, which support the fulfilment of primary activities.

Similarly, we assume that the value-added processes in a firm can generally be classified in three broad categories of significant processes (cf. Fig. 20):[49]

- management processes;
- business processes; and
- support processes

These three process categories consist, in turn, of a series of important subprocesses, which in total constitute the *process architecture*[50] of a firm. But what do these three process categories mean in detail?

Business processes concern the practical fulfilment of *core market-related activities* of a firm which are directly concerned with *creating customer benefit*.

Support processes provide the infrastructure and the provision of internal services necessary for business processes to be carried out effectively and efficiently.

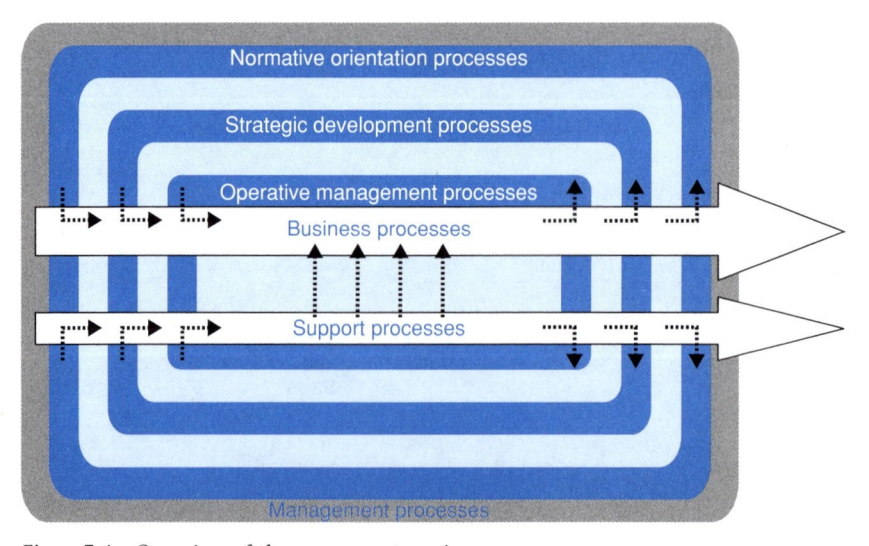

Figure 7.4 Overview of the process categories

Management processes embrace all of the fundamental management tasks concerned with designing, controlling (guiding) and developing a purpose-oriented socio-technical organisation (H. Ulrich, 1984). In other words, the *work of managing the firm* – regardless of who might perform this – is carried out in different management processes. Included in this work are all of the activities accompanying the planning, coordinating, quality assurance, and control activities of the individual *business* and *support processes*.

An example will briefly illustrate these three categories. An important task of a specially trained sales team in a pharmaceutical firm is to visit doctors systematically. This is an attempt to form a bond between doctors and the firm by informing, educating, and training them on the latest drugs and forms of therapy:

- Planning, coordinating and determining the effectiveness of the individual visits to the doctors by the sales team represents a *management process*.
- Actually carrying out the visits, the ensuing conversations, instructions, and distributing samples as well as analysing and evaluating these conversations represent a *business process*.
- A *support process* is represented by providing laptops with tailor-made customer relationship management software to register and update customer contacts, including important discussion themes, agreements, and feedback, and setting up a company-wide network so that the collected data may be recalled efficiently.

The following pages discuss these three main process categories in detail.

7.3.1 Management processes

As already mentioned, management processes cover all of the fundamental management tasks concerned with *designing, controlling (guiding) and developing a purpose-oriented socio-technical organisation* (H. Ulrich, 1984). Within these, we can distinguish between three central generic categories of management processes:

- normative orientation processes;
- strategy development processes;
- operative management processes.

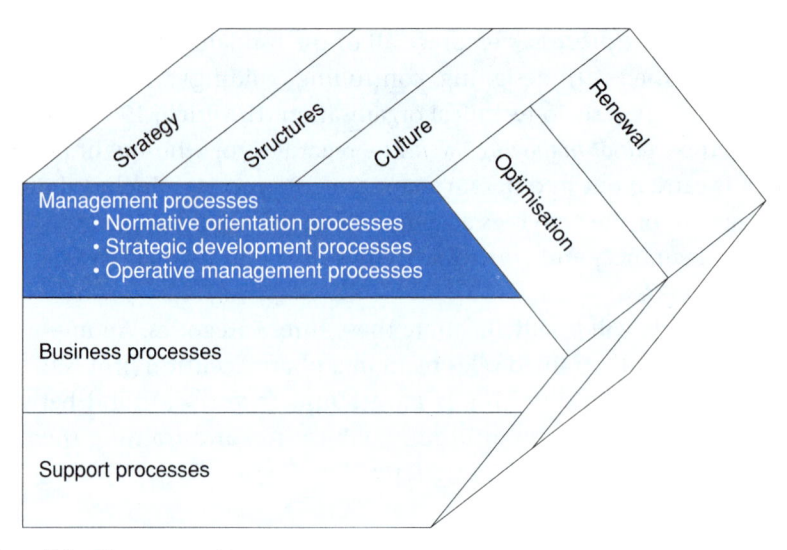

Figure 7.5 Management processes

Before we discuss these three categories, we should, first of all, briefly introduce the terms normative, strategic and operative. These three terms characterise the basic scope and decision areas of management (cf. Fig. 22 and P. Ulrich and Fluri, 1995, p. 19).

- The term *operative* refers to the *immediate resolution of day-to-day business*, with particular emphasis on the degree of efficiency with which limited resources are utilised.
- The term *strategic* refers to *securing the long-term competitive success of a firm*. There is thus a particular emphasis on responsiveness, in other words, how firms experience and react to market signals and to trends in individual environmental spheres affecting competition.
- The term *normative* refers to the *ethical legitimacy of a firm's business activity*. Therefore, there is a particular emphasis on a firm's responsiveness towards the ethical foundation of society and on its recognition of basic moral values and norms.

Thus the individual management processes can be understood as follows:

- In *normative orientation processes*, the normative foundation of business activity is contemplated and clarified (cf. also Chapters 4 and 5). This can involve, for example, by devising a code of conduct

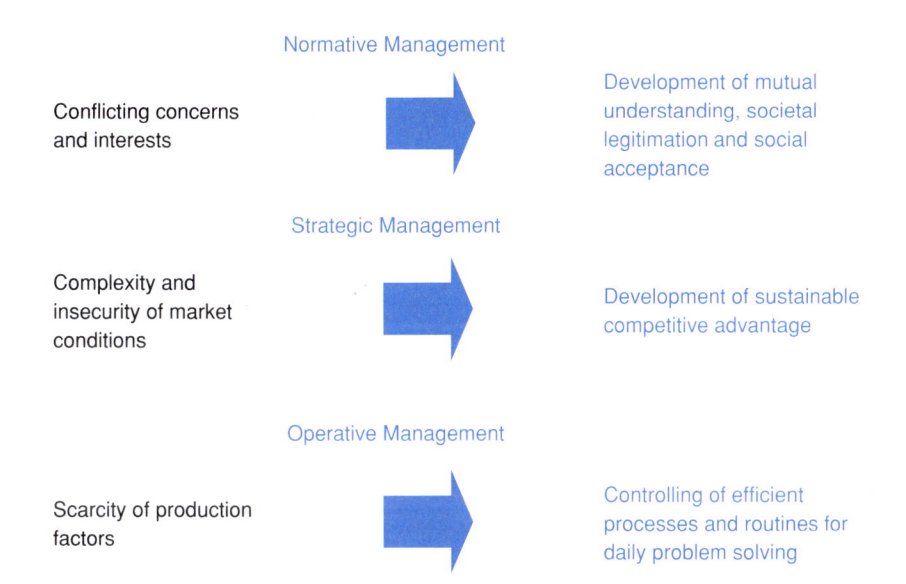

	Normative Management	
Conflicting concerns and interests	→	Development of mutual understanding, societal legitimation and social acceptance
	Strategic Management	
Complexity and insecurity of market conditions	→	Development of sustainable competitive advantage
	Operative Management	
Scarcity of production factors	→	Controlling of efficient processes and routines for daily problem solving

Source: Drawing closely on P. Ulrich and Fluri, 1995, p. 19.
Figure 7.6   Dimensions of management

in dealing with various stakeholder groups in cases of conflicting concerns and interests or in using risky technologies.
- *Strategy development processes* consist of all activities that lead to the development of a workable strategy as well as this strategy's successful implementation. They include careful change management and facilitation efforts to implement the intended changes into the firm's future daily operations (Müller-Stewens and Lechner, 1999, 2003). Therefore, strategy development processes include the development of new business models, *new process architecture* and *new process structures* (Section 7.4.1) or the initiation of strategic alliances, or even mergers and acquisitions (Section 6.3.3).
- By utilising *key performance indicators*, *operative management processes* consist in part of the *management of processes* in the individual business and support processes (cf. Section 7.4.2). There are, moreover, the following three management processes:
  - Processes of *leading people* help to establish a supportive working context and to develop constructive teamwork and goal-orientated behaviour of employees. This can happen in a number of ways, for example, by including employees in setting goals, in information, in how the workplace should be structured and tasks allocated, in training, in constructive feedback, etc.

- Processes of *financial controlling* serve the purpose of:
  (a) interpreting, evaluating and presenting the *financial implications* of management decisions and business transactions, with special reports targeted at various audiences. The controlling department thus plays a central role in this.
  (b) *controlling* and *reporting*, including performance evaluation and presentation of financial results to internal and external stake holders (investor relations).
  (c) *procuring capital* and optimising asset and liability management by considering risk and expected cash flows (including deci sions concerning capital expenditures).
  (d) processes of *quality management* involve appropriately defining (e.g., with support of delivery agreements) and timely fulfilling expectations of all parties concerned (external and internal customers and suppliers) in the individual management, business and support processes.

Within every management process, there is ideally–typically a sequence of four subprocesses, called *orientation, planning, implementation* and *feedback*, as illustrated in Fig. 23. *Orientation* involves contemplating and generating ideas and a sense of purpose. *Planning* concerns the identification of concrete goals and the binding agreement of goals. *Implementation* involves transferring the goals into everyday activities and routines in the firm. *Feedback* concerns closing this control circle with a loop of institutionalised feedback.

Furthermore, *basic attitudes* and *conduct* of the executives play a decisive role in all of the subprocesses.

7.3.2 Business processes

Business processes encapsulate the practical fulfilment of a firm's core market-related activities that are directly aimed at creating benefits for customers. We can distinguish between three significant process categories, which are strongly interconnected with each other in the everyday running of a firm:

- There are three subprocesses belonging to the *customer processes*: *customer acquisition, customer retention,* and *brand management*.[51] All of these processes ultimately lead to the customer's *decision to buy*

Feedback	►(p)review:	Ideas	Reflect, orientate, establish a common picture, gather ideas, and together explore new perspectives ► Willingness for self-criticism, creativity, openness
	▼ plan:	Goals	Select and prioritise ideas, define common goals and define activities, integrate these into an ordered and chronologically coherent framework, 'contracting' ► Willingness for commitment, honesty, flexibility
	▼ do:	Implementation	Implement agreed activities and innovations with commitment, and systematically learn from experience ► Willingness for change, loyalty, self-discipline

Figure 7.7 Control cycle as core leadership task of all of management processes

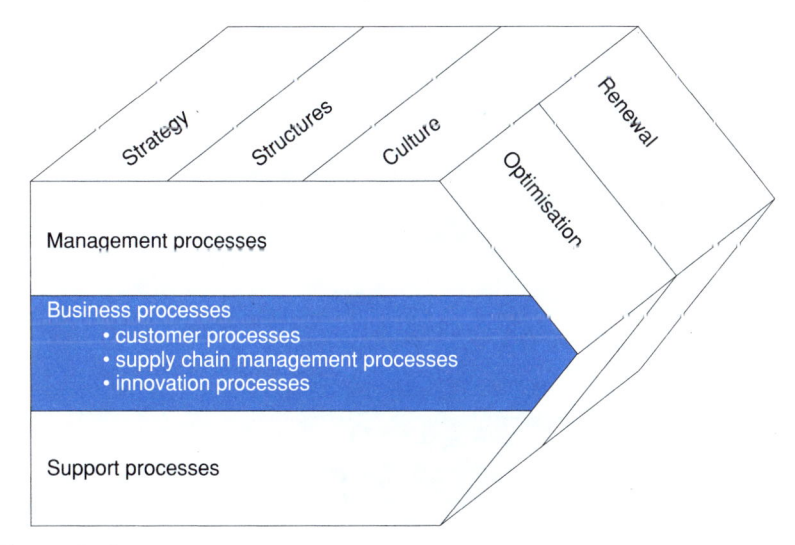

Figure 7.8 Business processes

(completion of the contract). In other words, this involves, for example, the tasks of market research, promotion activities, the development of communicative relationships with potential customers (customer acquisition) as well as developing and enhancing the relationship with acquired customers (customer loyalty and retention, customer relationship management).
- *Supply chain management processes* include all of the activities which lead to the customer receiving the agreed work with the agreed quality. The subprocesses *order fulfilment, procurement, logistics* and *production* are elements of this process.
- Finally, *innovation processes* include all of the subprocesses which contribute to systematic product and service innovation. Thus within industrial goods, the areas of *research* and *development* play a central role.

We characterise *core processes* as those business processes which, from the customer's point of view, provide a *superior customer benefit* compared competitors.

7.3.3 Support processes

Support processes serve to make the infrastructure available and to provide the necessary internal services so that business processes can be

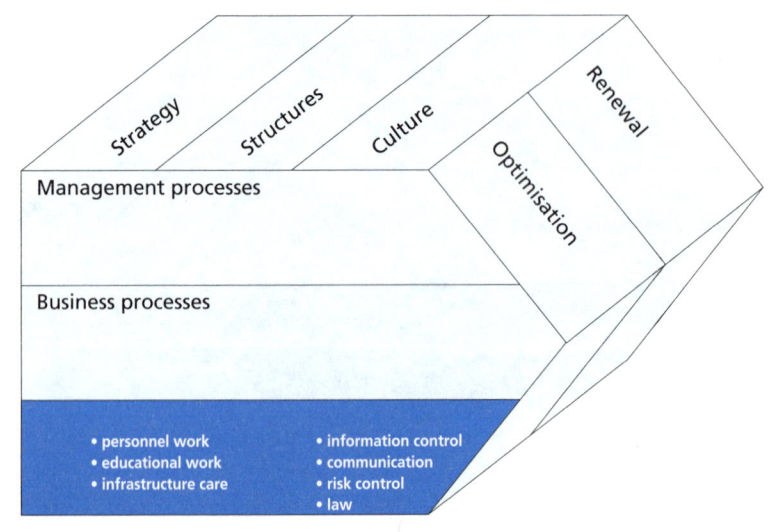

Figure 7.9   Support processes

accomplished effectively and efficiently. Support processes comprise the following subprocesses:

- *Personnel work* processes concern the *hiring, development, evaluation* and appropriate *compensation* of employees (Hilb, 1997).
- *Educational work* processes concern *systematically* providing employees with the opportunity for *further qualification* and establishing of a *progressive teach–learn–culture* in a firm.
- *Infrastructure care* processes concern the provision of cost-effective maintenance for the variety of infrastructure facilities.
- *Information control* processes concern the procurement of information technology (hardware and software) to provide *company data, financial data, risk data*, and data with respect to *key performance indicators* for the purpose of process management.
- *Communication* processes concern the development and support of supportive relationships with the external and internal stakeholders, going far beyond the pursuit of immediate economic interests (corporate identity, public relations). This particularly concerns the professional and communicative management of crises (issues management).
- *Risk control* processes concern appropriately evaluating and handling market-related, financial, technical and communicative risks that can arise in business activities.
- Processes of *law* concern providing a meaningful legal structure and legal support for business activities, ranging from stakeholders' legal entitlements to questions of optimising tax payments.

These support processes (just like the business processes) are designed, developed and controlled by management processes, i.e. by *human resource management, educational management, facility management, information management, communication management, risk management* and *legal management* (management of legal responsibilities), respectively

7.4 Management tasks in process management

Business processes and support processes require active *process management*. This forms part of the management processes.[52] There are, as already outlined briefly in Section 7.2, two distinct areas of responsibility: process *development* and process *control*.

In terms of the fundamental decisions in a firm, such as how to deal with the concerns and interests of different stakeholders, the tasks of developing and controlling processes are to guarantee or facilitate business success, i.e. ensuring a superior benefit for external stakeholders compared to competitors. This constitutes the central basis for a firm's long-term strategic success.

7.4.1 *Strategic* process management: process *development*

The tasks involved in *process development* form a subprocess of the *strategy development process*. This involves *fundamental arrangements* concerning the structure of *process architecture*, the *process structures* of individual business and support processes, and the definition of *key success factors* so that process quality can be assessed (Österle, 1995; Müller, 1999). In terms of a strategy development process, the duties involved in developing processes are largely the responsibility of one or more strategy teams.

The duties involved in developing processes are not, however, confined to technocratically planning specific structural arrangements. On the contrary, the development of processes involves an extremely demanding *multi-dimensional development process*. Its purpose is to develop a superior *process competency*, deeply affecting the structures, daily routines, technologies, culture and skill base of the employees. It is, therefore, primarily concerned with developing new *core competencies* or, in other words, strategically decisive collective capabilities.

7.4.2 *Operative* process management: process *control*

In contrast to the process development, the tasks of *process control* belong to *operative management processes*. Closer inspection reveals that process control involves the following tasks:

- First, everyday concerns of the firm, which cannot be structurally addressed and thus anticipated by process development, must be *addressed individually* and according to the situation – almost in a sense of fine-tuning.
- Secondly, processes normally involve completing an entire 'portfolio' of jobs or projects which are competing for limited resources. A *triage* is therefore necessary. This means prioritising and specifically allocating resources to individual jobs or projects. Additionally then, process control (in the sense of an active portfolio

management) must determine the *criteria*, which it will use to make ongoing decisions about which jobs and projects to be included and then prioritise these in the current working portfolio. These criteria will facilitate how to make the best possible alignment of tasks and resources over the course of time. Traditionally, the task of completing jobs and allocating resources has largely been characterised as *disposition*.
- Thirdly, ensuring the *quality* of a process also falls under the responsibility of process control. This involves repeatedly defining concrete objectives in terms of the specific key success factors used to measure process quality. It also involves checking whether these objectives are met or not and then employing appropriate measures in order to optimise the process and to improve the process quality. In other words, process control involves *continually optimising* processes without, however, needing to constantly re-examine fundamental arrangements.

These three tasks often fall under the responsibility of a *process team*, led by a *process owner* who is responsible for the specific process in question. Additionally, the task of optimising processes often falls under the responsibility of a quality circle or a CIP-team (CIP stands for continuous improvement process) which is ideally cross-functional in nature.

7.5 Interactions between structuring forces and processes

In Sections 2.3 and 6.6 we learnt that every firm is characterised by certain structuring forces, i.e. by particular characteristics of strategy, of structures and of culture. These *structuring forces* enable a coherent form to the daily stream of organisational activities, imposing upon it a certain order and thus more or less effectively directing daily activities towards the achievement of certain effects and results.

In the new St. Gallen Management Model, the daily stream of organisational activities is expressed in the *processes* of a firm. Processes are formed, more precisely, structured and guided, by structuring forces. But how are structuring forces generated? How are we to understand the interaction between *structuring forces* and *processes*, e.g. between a strategy development process (a subprocess of management processes) and a strategy?

Strategising work as the key ingredient of a strategy development process (management process), is not left to chance. On the contrary, it

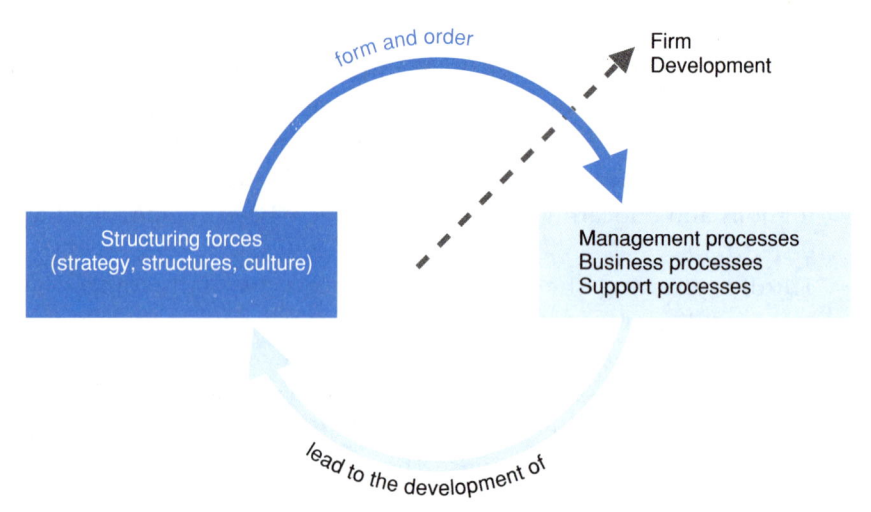

Figure 7.10 Circular (recursive) interaction of structuring forces and management processes

largely follows certain *procedural patterns* that can be traced back to a firm's already existing strategy, structures and culture, i.e. the structuring forces, which have developed in a firm's past and have more or less proved their worth.

The result of a strategy development process is a reworked and, ideally, an implemented strategy with appropriate structures and a specific culture. This in turn will become itself a crucial structuring force, enabling *in the future* to guide the daily stream of organisational activities in a firm towards achieving goals that have been recognised as proper and legitimate, goals that perhaps already exist or perhaps completely new ones. Furthermore, it will influence succeeding strategy development processes.

Looking at it from this perspective, we can thus see a *circular interaction* between structuring forces and business processes (especially the management processes) in a firm. This is because structuring forces (strategy, structures, culture) can always be seen as both the *media* (in the sense of 'structuring aids') for ordering daily organisational activities as well the *results* of these daily organisational activities.[53]

8
Modes of Firm Development: *Organisational Change*

These days, executives often lament the inevitability of change, yet, paradoxically, change is in fact a *prerequisite for stability*, as the famous cybernetic expert Ross Ashby (1956/1970) had already clearly demonstrated years ago with the example of riding in a straight line on a bicycle. He showed that fixing the handlebars of a bicycle would always quickly result in the cyclists falling, because he would be prevented from adjusting his bicycle to the large or small bumps along the way.

A successful firm development must, therefore, be characterised in a similar fashion by both stability and change, by uncertainty and renewed certainty, by upholding traditions and by boldly blazing new trails.

8.1 Analytical–technical and cultural–relational dimension of organisational change

Change in a firm usually affects two dimensions: on the one hand, the *analytical–technical dimension* (or functional logic), which deals with the contents and the functions of a firm's business activities; and on the other hand, the far less concrete *cultural–relational dimension* (or relational logic).

```
                                Business processes, procedural        Analytical–
                                routines and activity patterns        technical
                            ➜ along the value chain                   dimension

Organisational
Change
                                'Sense of belonging', identity,
                                basic attitudes, forms and quality
                                of relationships, interaction         Cultural–
                                partners, interactive patterns and    relational
                                routines                              dimension

                            ➜ along the organisational
                                interfaces of cooperation
```

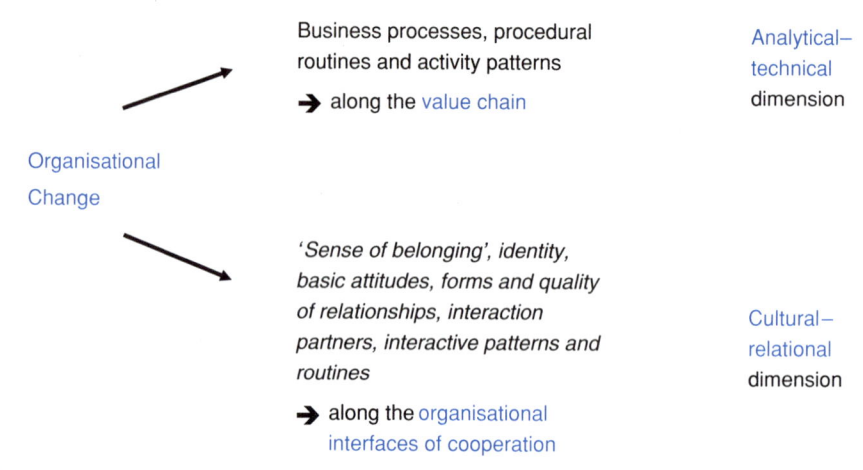

Figure 8.1 Analytical–technical and cultural–relational dimension of organisational change

Changes in terms of the *analytical–technical dimension* denote a change in organisational routines, in other words, activities and their normal order – often with the aid of new technology. Certain activities might be discarded, others preferred, no longer running sequentially, but accomplished in parallel or pushed to the back of the queue. Subtasks in the production process might be outsourced to suppliers, while at the same time integrating these suppliers deeper into processes of product innovation. Such changes can affect data and material flows, the employees' job descriptions, the workspace design, the schedule for accomplishing work, and the related need for flexibility to a greater or lesser degree. Changes in terms of the analytical–technical dimension can be analysed relatively easily and objectively by using techniques of process mapping.

In contrast, changes in terms of the *cultural–relational dimension* often involve wide-sweeping change in the following areas:

- a *sense of belonging to* as well as *relationships* (to a team, a department or the firm as a whole), and closely tied to this a sense of personal and collective *identity*;
- *values* and *opportunities for gaining a sense of identification*;
- *behaviour* and *attitudes*, in other words, the *basic assumptions* and *deeply held beliefs* of important people, groups of people, organisational units or organisations in a professional context

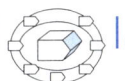

- employees' habits ('relational practices') deemed to be normal and appropriate with respect to teamwork, leadership and collaboration with other *people* and other *institutions* (e.g. teams, departments) within and outside of a firm.[54]

Attempts to implement New Public Management in the realm of governmental bureaucracies to make administrative work more efficient would not only involve, for example, the possibility of submitting a tax declaration directly via the Internet (analytical-technical dimension). It should also improve the quality of the relationship between the tax authorities and the citizens, for instance, if either party should need to follow up to clear up confusion.

8.2 Degree of organisational change

Change can take on different forms according to the following three categories:[55]

1. With respect to the *scope (breadth) of change*, the following question arises: how many areas of responsibility, fields of activity, processes and people will all together be affected by change in one way or another? Will change in effect be all-embracing, or will it involve a highly specific concentration on individual fields of activity or processes?
2. With respect to the *scale (depth) of change*, the following question arises: from the point of view of the people involved, how superficial or thorough will the changes be in the *structural arrangements*, in *cultural basic assumptions* and in the *organisational routines* of the firm's daily business activities? Are we talking about a slight 'fine-tuning' or a fundamental change?
3. With respect to the *intensity (speed) of change*, the following question arises: what is the time frame of implementation of these changes? Do employees get an occasional rest period or will they rarely experience periods of stability?

All in all, we can assert that the *broader, more thorough* and *quicker* the change, or in other words, the wider the *scope*, the greater the *consequences* and the higher the *intensity* of change, then, the more *fundamental* or *radical* will the corresponding change be in the firm.

8.3 Optimisation and renewal

In the development of many firms, more *evolutionary* and *incremental* phases alternate with more *revolutionary* and *radical* phases. In other words, phases of *continuous optimisation* are from time to time followed by phases of *fundamental renewal*.

This differentiation between evolutionary and revolutionary processes of change is very closely related to the second descriptive category, which covers the *scale* and the *profundity* of change. It is expressed in the Management Model by the important differentiation between *optimisation* and *renewal*.[56]

While *optimisation* can merely be compared with fine-tuning within given structures, *renewal* implies the *fundamental change* of a *pattern*, whether this involves (collective) *ways of thinking and interpretation*, *behavioural patterns* or *organisational routines*. Optimisation takes place when people can easily recognise their own areas of responsibility after a change has occurred. When, on the other hand, it is relatively difficult to recognise the evolved and familiar reality, then, there is a *point of rupture*, beyond which the usual processes and ways of thinking take on a *basic new form*, a new quality.

It is not easy to determine empirically whether a firm is undergoing optimisation or renewal. Determining this may be facilitated by the following framework with its five reference points (categories) for *firm development* (Fig. 30).

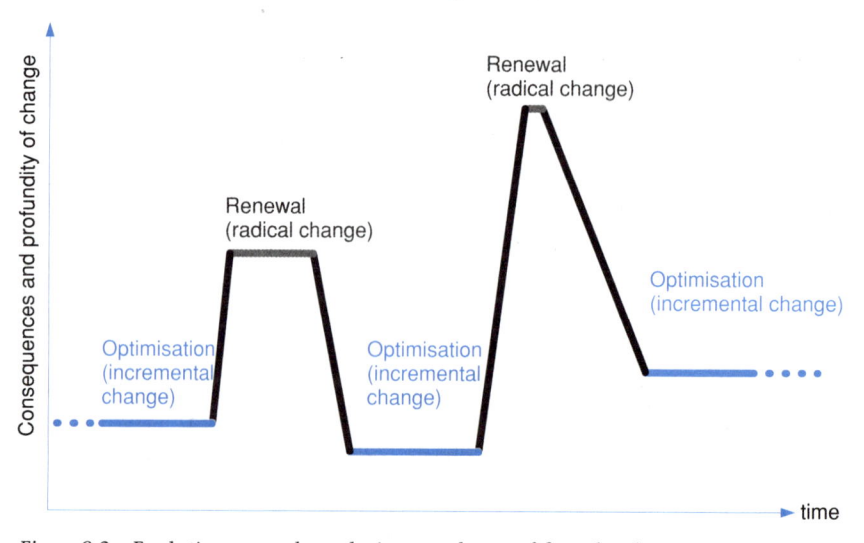

Figure 8.2 Evolutionary and revolutionary phases of firm development

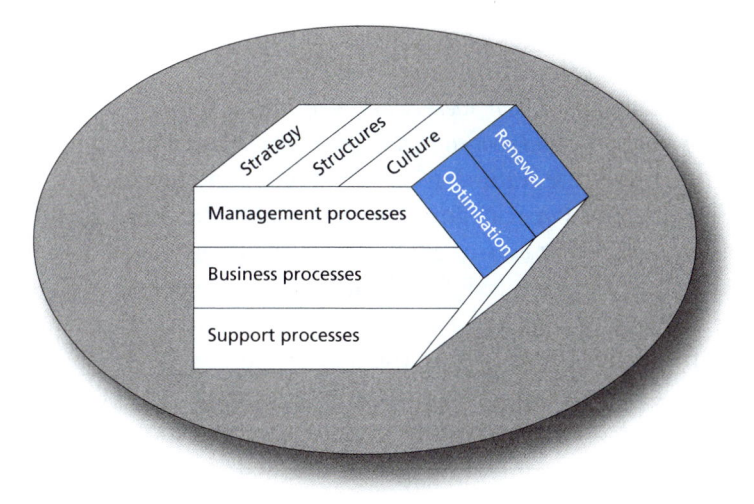

Figure 8.3 Optimisation and renewal as basic modes of firm development

Normative orientation processes and *strategy development processes* have a profound impact on *collective basic assumptions*, i.e. the *shared identity*, and, therefore, also on the *shared sense of purpose*. The emergence of new *discourses, ways of thinking and interpreting* largely indicate renewal, because they are usually associated with fundamental changes in other categories.

An extremely crucial reference point for all firm activities is the *firm purpose*, its crucial task – or in other words the 'mission' – and,

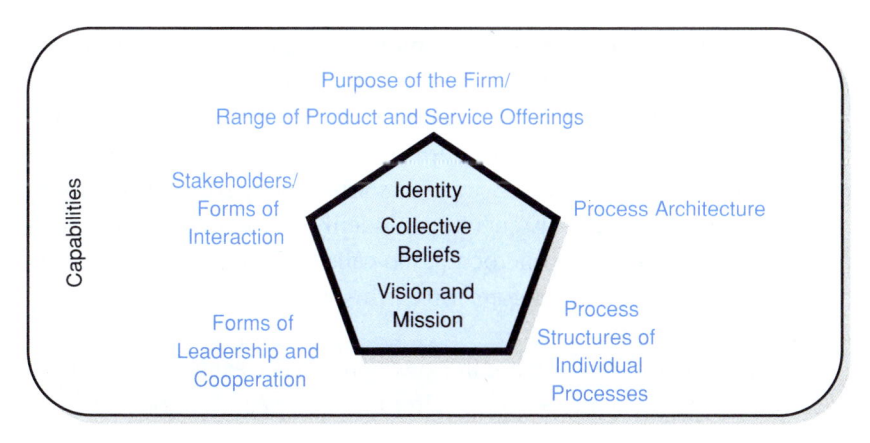

Figure 8.4 Reference points for firm development

in particular, the products and services it provides. This purpose has a powerful effect of creating a sense of identity.

Both the category *stakeholders – forms of interaction* and the category *practices of leadership and cooperation* express important starting points for change in terms of the cultural–relational dimension of change.

In contrast, the two categories *process architecture* and the *process patterns of individual processes* are based on relatively easily observable *procedural patterns* within individual value creation processes. Whenever a *firm's portfolio of products and services* is fundamentally changed, a need to fundamentally redefine the *process patterns* of the individual value creation processes mostly arises. The interactions between individual value creation processes represent the *process architecture* as a whole, which thus must also be redesigned. Redesigning the value creation processes, however, must not automatically lead to fundamental changes in the portfolio of products and services provided by the firm or even in its collective identity.

In general, *optimisation* means simply that these five categories have been harmonised more than before. By contrast, *renewal* has happened:

when *fundamental* changes emerge in at least one category, which then also significantly affect the other categories and their *harmonisation*; and

- when these changes are also linked to the development of fundamentally *new capabilities*.

It is precisely both this development of new collective (and this always means also new personal) *capabilities* and the closely associated development of new organisational routines, that imply that *renewal* usually embodies *strategic change*, enabling the accumulation of new core competencies and the development of fundamentally different relationship to the environment and its stakeholders.

Nevertheless, great things can also be accomplished with continuous optimisation. We need only to think of the Swiss clock-making and watch-making industry, which for years strove to perfect mechanical clockworks until its very existence was suddenly threatened in the seventies by the development of microchips. So-called 'disruptive technologies' (Christensen, 1997) can, therefore, force firms into a fundamental renewal overnight.

Optimisation and renewal are in no way mutually exclusive. Often in one firm, renewal is required for certain processes, departments and areas of activity, while for others optimisation is entirely sufficient. Ultimately, it is those firms that are adept at combining both optimisation and renewal that are best able to continuously develop.

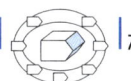

By using quality circles (Imai, 1989) or 'Continuous Improvement Process Teams,' optimisation can almost run parallel to the work of meeting everyday business activities. However, sustainable renewal requires ways of institutionalising the work needed to implement change. This includes more or less comprehensive forms of project management (Heintel and Krainz, 1994) or the creation of an actual 'arena of change', that is an organisation of change within the firm,[57] which develops innovations, continuously introduces and implements them, reinforces them and finally fits them into the day-to-day work of the firm's employees.

Renewal, in the sense of strategic change, is linked with the *development of new core competencies* and thus also very frequently with sweeping *efforts towards further qualification*. It is, therefore, advisable not to attempt to change everything all at once, especially in the light of the interplay between stability and change. Otherwise, a situation can develop which the protagonists of change will quickly describe as 'resistance'.[58] However, the employees of a company and the firm as a whole must again and again be able to 'digest' change. This sometimes necessitates a *sequencing* of change over the course of time (in the sense of Fig. 28) (Wimmer, 1999). Additionally, a successful renewal will always need islands of stability, shelters of certainty and phases of consolidation, even when much in a firm is interwoven and interdependent.

Obviously, not all firms share equally suitable prerequisites to cope with change. Dealing with the interplay of stability and change within the framework of the firm's ability to change and renew is one of the most challenging tasks of management – both in a strategic as well as in an ethical sense.

9
Epilogue: Reinventing the Wheel?

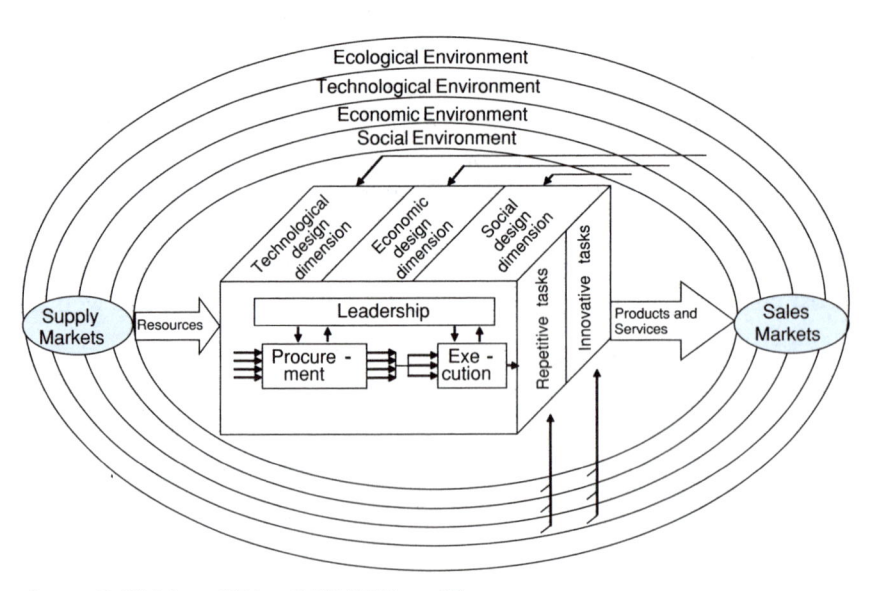

Source: H. Ulrich and Krieg (1972/1974, p. 27).
Figure 9.1 Management model of the first St. Gallen Management Model and the new St. Gallen Management Model in comparison (opposite page)

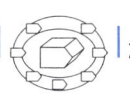

At this point, the critical question may rightly be posed: what is so new about this Management Model? Does it come down to nothing more than new fads and myths (Kieser, 1996)? A glance at the first version of the St. Gallen Management Model from the 1970s, in fact, shows that the new edition can be understood as an organic evolution.

The following have become more important:

- a systematic examination of the *normative foundations of business management*, i.e. the norms and values;
- a clear awareness of the *stakeholders* of a firm with their various concerns, interests and demands;
- a careful consideration of the subtle interplay between *strategy, structures* and the much more intangible, but equally important *culture* of a firm;
- the significance of the *time* factor with a the consequence to focus all its value-added activities towards stakeholders using clearly structured *processes*;
- a far broader understanding of *resources* (compared to the 'means' of the procurement market).

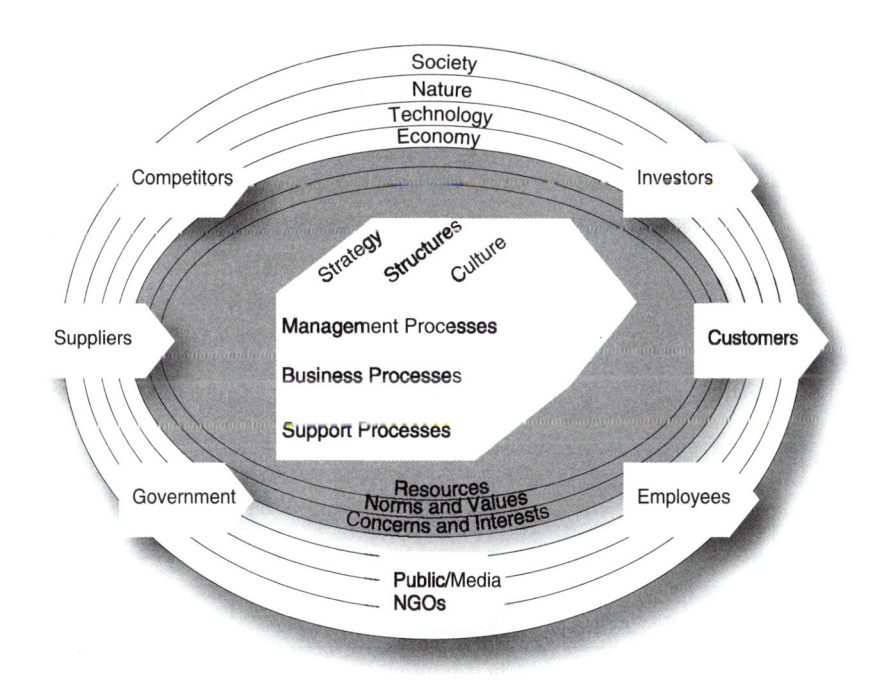

This extension of the management model should not, however, obscure the fact that the truly significant ideas and maxims of our culture tend to have much older roots than we generally assume. This is particularly true in the context of the prevailing dynamic and hectic nature of modern times and in the context of the old adage 'the only certainty is change'. Through careful source studies in the St. Gallen monastic library, the Mannheim-based organisational researcher Alfred Kieser convincingly demonstrated in the 1980s[59] that nearly all consistently successful modern principles of management and organisation can be traced back to the organisation of medieval monastic life. Therefore, monasteries can be considered as the first modern organisations.

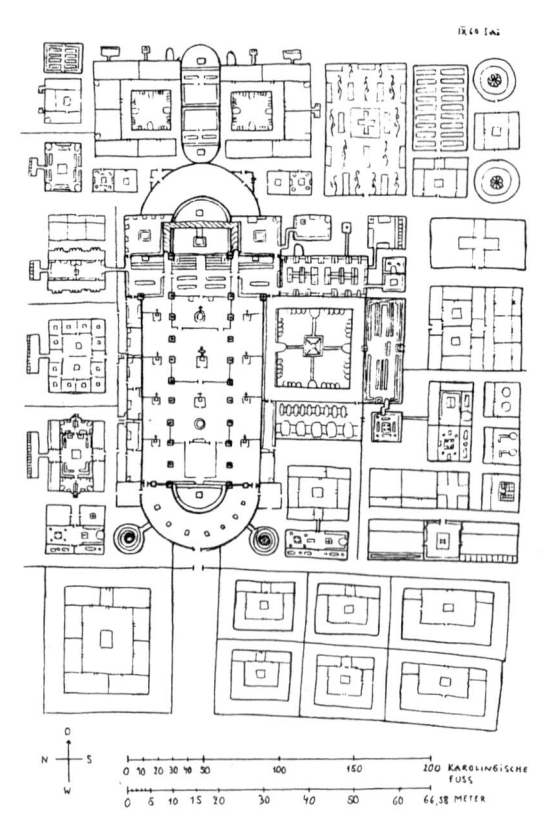

Figure 9.2   The blueprint for the St. Gallen Carolingian monastery, designed and labelled around 819/830 in the Reichenau monastery

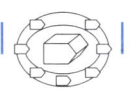

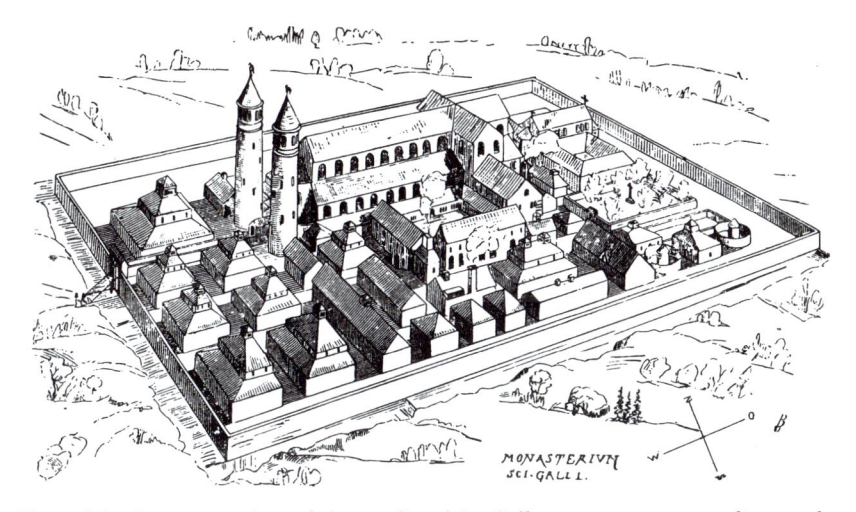

Figure 9.3 Reconstruction of the medieval St. Gallen monastery according to the blueprint of the St. Gallen monastery

Quite surprisingly, then, historical writings from the St. Gallen monastery, and in particular the eighth-century construction blueprint (from a historical point of view the first ever documented), can indicate a series of practices, the application of which remains very current to this very day, for instance:

- *rules* being a methodological basic element for an organisation based on the *division of labour*;
- written and *fixed rules of work* (passed down by God in the sense of a code of conduct and of statements in a quality handbook);
- principles of a *process-oriented* division of labour aimed at attaining a clearly structured and optimised; workflow (process orientation) with an appropriate production layout (see the monastery plan);
- *strict time management* as the basis for an routinisation of work processes;
- *job rotation* as an element of humanising the work;
- the beginnings of modern *accounting* with planning and reporting;
- principles of *clearly regulated corporate governance* (with the abbot as 'Chief Executive Officer,' the treasurer as the 'Chief Financial Officer' and the 'cellarer' as the 'Controller');

- principles of systematic *knowledge sharing,* that is disseminating proven solutions (in a network of friendly monasteries) and much more.

Thus, the circle is closed by passing from the new St. Gallen Management Model at the beginning of the 21st century back in time to the monastic culture of the eighth century, which even today can be admired in the St. Gallen monastic library.

Notes

1. Cf. Reckwitz (1997).
2. Cf. for example, Berger and Luckmann (1966) and Weick (1979).
3. As an illustration, if we can improve the educational qualifications of the employees [criterion people] through company training, then this has a positive effect on the quality of the processes [criterion processes], which in turn leads to higher customer satisfaction [criterion customer results] as well as higher employee satisfaction [criterion people results] on account of reducing conflicts and finally to improved business results [criterion key performance results].
4. Cf. in detail Anderegg (1985, pp. 55ff.).
5. The development of a certain linguistic tradition, a basis for thought and reason in the context of complex communicative and relational processes is embodied in a *discourse* (cf. in detail Burr, 1995).
6. Cf. in detail H. Ulrich (1968/1970, 1984, 1978/1987); Luhmann (1984); Willke (1996a, b); Rüegg-Stürm (1998, 2001); Simon (2001).
7. Cf. in detail von Hayek (1972); Malik (1984/2002); Simon (2001).
8. In this text, the notion of *structuration* is understood in the sense of Giddens (1984).
9. This term was coined by Brown and Duguid (1991) and Wenger (1998) to describe an organisation as a *community of communities-of-practice*.
10. The term 'organisation' is more broadly defined than 'firm'. It also encompasses other institutions which are based on the division of labour, such as the ICRC, hospitals, public authorities, church organisations, trade unions or football clubs.
11. NGOs (in the stakeholder category, at the bottom-middle of the model) are defined as Non Governmental Organisations. These are gaining increasing importance in political debates.
12. The term *structuring forces* draws heavily upon Giddens's term *structural properties* (cf. in detail Giddens, 1984, pp. 185ff.). In this sense, structuring forces mean an embracing, ordering and structuring 'factor,' comparable to the structure (grammar, semantics) of a language.
13. In contrast, the central principle in the strategic concept of stakeholders is the question, what kind of stakeholders, on the one hand, and the firm, on the other hand, to which extent are able to mobilise and *use power* in order to (politically) *enforce* their interests.
14. The Nobel Prize winner Milton Friedman expressed this very vividly in 1962: 'There is one and only one social responsibility of business – to use its resources and engage in activities designed to increase its profits so long as it stays within the rules of the game, which is to say, engages in open and free competition without deception or fraud.'
15. Cf. in more detail P. Ulrich (2001) and P. Ulrich (2004).
16. Cf. in detail Dyllick (1989).

17. *Demands* on a firm might be rooted either more in general value-based concerns or more in self interest.
18. Cf. in more detail P. Ulrich (2001) and P. Ulrich (2004).
19. This element illustrates just how problematic the notion of Human *Resource* Management is in terms of our desire for a holistic business management. For when we talk of the added value of *people,* we are *not* dealing with objectified, commercial resources, but expressions of human activity and culture.
20. The difference outlined here between establishing orientation, coordination and meaning in a firm draws heavily on Frost (1998) and Osterloh (1999), who differentiate between *tools of orientation, coordination* and *motivation* in an organisation.
21. The famous distinction between 'doing the *right* things' and 'doing things *right*' was coined by the management pioneer Peter Drucker (1966, p. 12).
22. The development of a shared sense of purpose for the members of a firm does not only have strategic importance but it is also an important task of *normative orientation processes.*
23. Cf. in detail Burns (1961); Crozier and Friedberg (1977); Küpper and Ortmann (1986, 1988); Neuberger (1995); Sandner (1992).
24. This depth of production determines which part of the entire value creation chain an enterprise addresses itself. Thus, at the beginning of the century, Ford demonstrated a depth of production approaching 100%, in other words, Ford took on every activity itself, from extracting raw materials to assembly on the production line and delivery. In contrast, the Smart car encompasses a production level ranging from 15% to 20% and home computers (Dell, IBM) from 5% to 7%. This means that these firms source integrated business solutions from selected suppliers (business partners) and are themselves merely responsible for highly efficient logistics, assembly and marketing. The trend over time towards a *decreasing depth of production* is an indication of the increasing division of labour (levelling out) in the economy and society.
25. Segmentation always occurs when there is an intend to understand complex problems more thoroughly by breaking them down into their constituent parts and to analyse and handle these in a more targeted fashion (e.g. with marketing measures) (Müller-Stewens and Lechner, 2003). Segmentation occurs when there are specific criteria or characteristics and specific differentiation. For example, business areas can be segmented according to buyer industries (differentiating, for example, between the pharmaceutical industry, the cosmetics industry or the food industry), according to buyer regions (differentiating for example between Northern Europe, Central Europe, Southern Europe, Eastern Europe, North America, or the Far East), or according to sales channels (differentiating for example between direct sales, using sales channels or franchising).
26. In terms of *industrial–economic* considerations this perspective is also referred to as the *structure–conduct–performance* paradigm.
27. Cf. Penrose (1959) and Wernerfelt (1984).
28. A branch of science is conducting vigorous research into why businesses arise in the first place, and why all transactions do not take place directly through the market. This branch of science, the so-called *New Institutional Economics* (Coase, 1937; cf. for an overview Walter-Busch, 1996, pp. 287ff. and Ebers and Gotsch,

1999, pp. 199ff.), is posited between economics, especially micro-economics, and management studies.
29. Cf. in detail Probst (1987) and Baitsch (1993), as well as Section 6.5.2.
30. Cf. Weick (1979, pp. 18f.).
31. This process of *routinisation* (Giddens, 1984, pp. xxiiff. and 60ff) is explained in more detail in Section 6.6.
32. P. Ulrich (1984) and P. Ulrich (1990); for further reference to the term *business culture* see also Schein (1985); Lattmann (1990); Sackmann (1991); Martin (1992).
33. This idea is derived from Giddens's notion of a permanent process of *reflexive monitoring of action* (cf. in detail Giddens, 1984, particularly pp. 3ff. and 44).
34. 'It is normal for this to happen because …'.
35. 'It is right to do this because …'.
36. 'When X happens, I should always do Y.'
37. Elden (1983); cf. also Baitsch (1993) and Martin (1992, pp. 130ff). 'Local theories' are also described as locally valid 'thought worlds' (Dougherty, 1992a, b) or as 'local ontologies' (Gergen, 1995, pp. 38f. and 1999, pp. 81ff).
38. In this context, *self-referential* (recursive or reflexive) means that processes of structuration refer primarily to *conditions* and *contexts* which are enacted and reproduced simultaneously in these processes on an ongoing basis. From this theoretical perspective, it is not so much the freely selected individual goals, intentions, or motives of individuals (e.g. those of individual executives) that guide these processes and impose upon them a certain order. Instead, it is much more the organically developed contexts, i.e. the developed strategies, structures, communicative and relational processes which comprise the key structuring forces. In Anglo-Saxon literature this is known as 'path dependency.'
39. Giddens (1984) refers to this as the *duality of structure* (structuring forces) *and action* (organisational routines).
40. Cf. in detail Giddens (1984), in particular pp. xxiiff and 5ff.
41. This gives rise to the notion in Daft and Weick (1984) that businesses are systems of interpretation.
42. Cf. in detail Bateson (1972) and Frost (1998).
43. Cf. Prahalad and Bettis (1986) and Leonard-Barton (1992).
44. Cf. in detail Weick (1979, pp. 229, 249).
45. Cf. Becker, *et al.* (1999); Hammer (1996); Müller (1999); Osterloh and Frost (1998); Schuh, *et al.* (1998) and Servatius (1994).
46. Cf. in detail Fleisch (2001).
47. Cf. here in more detail Section 7.4.2.
48. We deliberately suggest a distinction here between the industry-specific value creation chain and the firm-specific value chain. The *value chain* of a firm includes all of the task areas and activities that comprise the *specific focus* of a firm's added value. By contrast, the *value creation chain* includes a wide range of activities and levels of added value throughout the *entire business* that are necessary for manufacturing a specific product. As an illustration, the value creation chain in textiles embraces all of the value-added activities from planting the cotton to the finished item of clothing in the clothes shop, including customer advice and customer serve. The value chain of a spinning mill embraces all of

the value-added activities from the delivery of the cotton to the delivery of the finished yarn to a weaving mill.
49. In their St. Gallen Management Model, Hans Ulrich and Walter Krieg (1972/1974, p. 23) have similarly distinguished between *leadership activities, fulfilment units* and *sourcing units*.
50. A *process architecture* contains different process categories. A process architecture can be broken up into different degrees of resolution (for example into a macro-perspective or into a micro-perspective), depending on whether a general overview is desired, or a more detailed look into individual process categories. In other words, there is a 'process hierarchy,' in which individual process categories can always be sub-divided into more detailed subprocesses (and finally into individual tasks).
51. Cf. in detail Bieger and Tomczak (2004) on this categorisation.
52. This should not obscure the fact that management processes themselves also require both careful process development (e.g. how should the process of developing a strategy be designed) and process control (e.g. how should the work of developing a strategy be coordinated).
53. These ideas are based on the Giddens' theory of structure (cf. in detail Giddens, 1984, pp. 185ff).
54. This type of change does *not* deal with – as is often postulated in practice – a 'change in the mind-sets of individual workers'. The central focus goes beyond individual change, to the level of cultural change, involving a shift in the *commonly experienced daily reality*. Figuratively speaking, such a cultural change can be compared with a change in the commonly employed 'grammar of an organisation'. This demonstrates clearly how demanding a successful cultural change will be.
55. Cf. in detail Kanter (1983); Kanter, *et al.* (1992); Reiss, *et al.* (1997).
56. This differentiation expresses a phenomenon which has already been described in a variety of ways. For example, as a *first-order change* as opposed to a *second-order change* (Watzlawick, *et al.* 1974), or *single-loop learning* as opposed to *double-loop learning* (Argyris and Schön, 1978), or *survival activities* as opposed to *advancement activities* (von Krogh and Roos, 1995).
57. Kanter (1983, pp. 200ff, especially pp. 204f. and pp. 359ff, 407) uses the terms *parallel organisation* or *secondary structure* for this. They have the particular purpose of enabling successful, cross-functionally integrated work.
58. Resistance is far from being a simple phenomenon that can be easily diagnosed. Resistance often describes the problematic behaviour of individuals or groups (e.g. 'the middle management') from the perspective of the protagonists of change. Resistance is frequently attributed to the particular modes of behaviour of certain individuals or groups. This attribution is a reaction to well or less well justified opposition, or to an offer by the critics of change to engage in dialogue, or to an often thoroughly understandable inhibition of certain individuals or groups. What might, however, be seen as resistance in the context of one 'local theory,' might in the context of another 'local theory' be understood as a constructive offer for dialogue or as a well justified, legitimate criticism. Thus, great care must be taken when dealing with the term resistance.
59. Cf. in detail Kieser (1986, 1989, 1992).

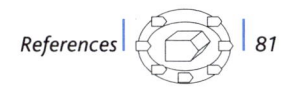

References

When there are 2 dates, the first year indicates the time of the first edition in its original version.

Abell, D. (1980) *Defining the Business: The Starting Point of Strategic Planning.* Englewood Cliffs: Prentice-Hall.

Anderegg, J. (1985) *Sprache und Verwandlung: Zur literarischen Ästhetik.* Göttingen: Vandenhoeck & Ruprecht.

Ansoff, I. (1984) *Implanting Strategic Management.* London: Prentice-Hall.

Argyris, Ch./Schön, D. (1978) *Organizational Learning: A Theory of Action Perspective.* Reading, MA: Addison-Wesley.

Ashby, R. (1956/1970): *An Introduction to Cybernetics.* 5th edn, London: Chapman and Hall.

Baitsch, Ch. (1993) *Was bewegt Organisationen?: Selbstorganisation aus psychologischer Perspektive.* Frankfurt: Campus.

Barney, J. (1991) 'Firm Resources and Sustained Competitive Advantage'. In: *Journal of Management*, 17, 1, 99–120.

Bateson, G. (1972) *Steps to an Ecology of Mind: Collected Essays in Anthropology, Psychiatry, Evolution and Epistemology.* London: Paladin.

Becker, J./Kugeler, M./Rosemann, M. (Hrsg) (1999) *Prozessmanagement: ein Leitfaden zur prozessorientierten Organisationsgestaltung.* Berlin: Springer.

Belz, Ch. (1997) Leistungssysteme. In: ders. (Hrsg.) *Leistungs- und Kundensysteme, Kompetenz für Marketing-Innovationen, Schrift* 2, St. Gallen: Thexis, 12–39.

Berger, P./Luckmann, Th. (1966) *The Social Construction of Reality.* New York: Doubleday.

Bieger, Th./Tomczak, Th. (2004) 'Geschäftsprozesse'. In: Dubs, R., Euler, D., Rüegg-Stürm, J. and Wyss, Ch. (Hrsg): *Einführung in die Managementlehre.* Bern: Haupt.

Bleicher, K. (1991/1999) *Das Konzept Integriertes Management. Visionen – Missionen – Programme.* 6. Auflage, Frankfurt: Campus.

Bleicher, K. (1994) *Normatives Management. Politik, Verfassung und Philosophie des Unternehmens.* Frankfurt: Campus.

Bogner, W./Thomas, H. (1994) 'Core Competence and Competitive Advantage: A Model and Illustrative Evidence from the Pharmaceutical Industry'. In: Hamel, G. and Heene, A. (eds): *Competence-based Competition.* Chichester. John Wiley, 111–44.

Brown, J./Duguid, P. (1991) 'Organizational Learning and Communities-of-Practice: Toward a Unified View of Working, Learning and Innovation'. In: *Organization Science*, 2, No. 1, 40–57.

Burns, T. (1961) 'Micropolitics: Mechanisms of Institutional Change'. In: *Administrative Science Quarterly*, 6, No. 3, 257–81.

Burr, V. (1995) *An Introduction to Social Constructionism.* London: Routledge.

Christensen, C. (1997) *The Innovator's Dilemma: When New Technologies Cause Great Firms to Fail.* Boston: Harvard Business School Press.

Coase, R. H. (1937) 'The Nature of the Firm'. In: *Economica*, N.S., 4, 386–405.
Crozier, M./Friedberg, E. (1977) *L'acteur et le système: Les constraintes de l'action collective*. Paris: Seuil.
Dachler, H. P. (1990) 'Führung und Organisation im Kontext kultureller und sprachlicher Vielfalt in zukünftigen Organisationen'. In: Bleicher, K. and Gomez, P. (Hrsg): *Zukunftsperspektiven der Organisation*. Bern: Stämpfli, 45–66.
Dachler, H. P. (1992) 'Management and Leadership as Relational Phenomena'. In: von Cranach, M., Doise, W. and Mugny, G. (eds): *Social Representations and the Social Basis of Knowledge*. Lewiston: Hogrefe & Huber, 169–78.
Daft, R. L./Weick, K. E. (1984) 'Toward a Model of Organizations as Interpretation Systems'. In: *Academy of Management Review*, 9, No. 2, 284–95.
Dougherty, D. (1992a) 'A Practice-centered Model of Organizational Renewal Through Product Innovation'. In: *Strategic Management Journal*, 13 Summer Special Issue, 77–92.
Dougherty, D. (1992b) 'Interpretative Barriers to Successful Product Innovation in Large Firms'. In: *Organization Science*, 3, No. 2, 179–202.
Drucker, P. (1966) *The Effective Executive*. New York: Harper & Row.
Dubs, R./Euler, D./Rüegg-Stürm, J./Wyss, Ch. (2004) *Einführung in die Managementlehre*. Bern: Haupt.
Dyllick, Th. (1989) *Management der Umweltbeziehungen*. Wiesbaden: Gabler.
Ebers, M./Gotsch, W. (1999) 'Institutionenökonomische Theorien der Organisation'. In: Kieser, A. (Hrsg): *Organisationstheorien*. 3. überarbeitete und erweiterte Aufl., Stuttgart: Kohlhammer, 199–251.
Elden, M. (1983) 'Democratization and Participative Research in Developing Local Theory'. In: *Journal of Occupational Behaviour*, 4, 21–33.
European Foundation for Quality Management (EFQM) (ed.) (2003) *Assessing for Excellence: A Practical Guide for Successfully Developing, Executing and Reviewing a Self-assessment Strategy for Your Organisation*. Brüssel: EFQM.
Fleisch, E. (2001) *Das Netzwerkunternehmen: Strategien und Prozesse zur Steigerung der Wettbewerbsfähigkeit in der 'Networked Economy'*. Berlin: Springer.
Freeman, R. E. (1984) *Strategic Management: A Stakeholder Approach*. Boston: Pitman.
French, W. L./Bell, C. H., Jr (1973) *Organization Development: Behavioural Science Interventions for Organization Improvement*. 5th edn. Englewood Cliffs: Prentice-Hall.
Frost, J. (1998) *Die Koordinations- und Orientierungsfunktion der Organisation*. Bern: Haupt.
Gergen, K. (1995) 'Relational Theory and the Discourses of Power'. In: Hosking, D., Dachler, H. P. and Gergen, K. (eds): *Management and Organization: Relational Alternatives to Individualism*. Aldershot: Avebury, 29–50.
Gergen, K. (1999) *An Invitation to Social Construction*. London: Sage.
Giddens, A. (1984) *The Constitution of Society: Outline of the Theory of Structuration*. Cambridge: Polity Press.
Gomez, P. (1981) *Modelle und Methoden des systemorientierten Managements*. Bern: Haupt.
Gomez, P. (1983) *Frühwarnung in der Unternehmung*. Bern: Haupt.
Gomez, P. (1999) *Integrated value management*. London: International Thomson Business Press.
Gomez, P./Probst, G. (1999) *Die Praxis des ganzheitlichen Problemlösens. 3. Auflage*, Bern: Haupt.

Hamel, G./Prahalad, C. (1994) *Competing for the Future*. Boston: Harvard Business School Press.
Hammer, M. (1996) *Beyond Engineering*. New York: Harper Collins.
von Hayek, F. A. (1972) *Theorie komplexer Phänomene*. Tübingen: Mohr.
Heintel, P./Krainz, E. (1994) *Projektmanagement*. 3. Auflage, Wiesbaden: Gabler.
Hilb, M. (1997) *Integriertes Personalmanagement: Ziele, Strategien, Instrumente*. 4. überarbeitete Auflage, Neuwied: Luchterhand.
Hosking, D./Dachler, H. P./Gergen, K. (eds) (1995) *Management and Organization: Relational Alternatives to Individualism*. Aldershot: Avebury.
Imai, M. (1989) *Kaizen: The Key to Japan's Competitive Success*. New York: McGraw-Hill.
Kanter, R. (1983) *The Change Masters*. New York: Simon & Schuster.
Kanter, R., Stein, B. and Jick, T. (eds) (1992) *The Challenge of Organizational Change*. New York: Free Press.
Kieser, A. (1986) 'Von asketischen zu industriellen Bravourstücken. Die Organisation der Wirtschaft im Kloster des Mittelalters'. In: *Mannheimer Berichte*, Nr. 30, Dezember 1986.
Kieser, A. (1989) 'Organizational, Institutional, and Societal Evolution: Medieval Craft Guilds and the Genesis of Formal Organizations'. In: *Administrative Science Quarterly*, 34, No. 4, 540–64.
Kieser, A. (1992) 'Organisationsstrukturen, historische Entstehung von'. In: Frese, E. (Hrsg): *Handwörterbuch der Organisation* (HWO). Stuttgart: C. E. Poeschel, Sp. 1648–70.
Kieser, A. (1996) 'Moden und Mythen des Organisierens'. In: *Die Betriebswirtschaft*, 56, Heft 1, 21–39.
Kieser, A. (1998) 'Über die allmähliche Verfertigung von Organisation beim Reden. Organisieren als Kommunizieren'. In: *Industrielle Beziehungen*, 5, Heft 1, 45–75.
Kirsch, W. (1990) *Unternehmenspolitik und strategische Unternehmensführung*. München: Barbara Kirsch.
von Krogh, G./Venzin, M. (1995) Wissensmanagement. In: *Die Unternehmung*, 49, Heft 6, 417–36.
von Krogh, G./Roos, J. (1995) *Organizational Epistemology*. London: Macmillan Press.
Küpper, W./Ortmann, G. (1986) 'Mikropolitik in Organisationen'. In: *Die Betriebswirtschaft*, 46, 5, 590–602.
Küpper, W./Ortmann, G. (Hrsg.) (1988) *Mikropolitik – Rationalität, Macht und Spiele in Organisationen*. Opladen: Westdeutscher Verlag.
Lattmann, Ch. (Hrsg.) (1990) *Unternehmenskultur*. Heidelberg: Physica.
Leonard-Barton, D. (1992) 'Core Capabilities and Core Rigidities. A Paradox in Managing New Product Development'. In: *Strategic Management Journal*, 13, Summer Special Issue, 111–25.
Luhmann, N. (1984) *Soziale Systeme. Grundlegung einer allgemeinen Theorie*. Frankfurt: Suhrkamp.
Malik, F. (1981) 'Management-Systeme'. In: *Die Orientierung*, Nr. 78, Bern: Schweizerische Volksbank.
Malik, F. (1984/2002) *Strategie des Managements komplexer Systeme*. 7. Auflage, Bern: Haupt.
Martin, J. (1992) *Cultures in Organizations: Three Perspectives*. New York: Oxford University Press.
Mintzberg, H. (1998) *Strategy Safari*. London: Prentice-Hall.

Morgan, G. (1997) *Images of Organization*. Beverly Hills: Sage.
Müller, M. (1999) *Prozessorientierte Veränderungsprojekte – Fallbeispiele des Unternehmenswandels*. Bamberg: difo.
Müller-Stewens, G./Lechner, Ch. (1999) 'Die Gestaltung unternehmerischer Einheiten: Der General Management Navigator als ein Konzept zur integrierten Strategie- und Wandelarbeit'. In: *Organisationsentwicklung*, 18, 2, 25–43.
Müller-Stewens, G./Lechner, Ch. (2003) *Strategisches Management: Wie strategische Initiativen zu Wandel führen*. 2. Auflage, Stuttgart: Schäffer-Poeschel.
Nalebuff, B./Brandenburger, A. (1996) *Co-opetition*. New York: Doubleday.
Nelson, R./Winter, S. (1982) *An Evolutionary Theory of Economic Change*. Cambridge, MA: Belknap.
Neuberger, O. (1995) *Mikropolitik: der alltägliche Aufbau und Einsatz von Macht in Organisationen*. Stuttgart: Enke.
Österle, H. (1995) *Business Engineering*. Berlin u.a.: Springer.
Osterloh, M. (1999) 'Märkte als neue Form der Organisation und Führung? Oder: Wann ist virtuell virtuous?' In: Gomez, P., Müller-Stewens, G. and Rüegg-Stürm, J. (Hrsg.): *Entwicklungsperspektiven einer integrierten Managementlehre*. Bern: Haupt, 381–408.
Osterloh, M./Frost, J. (1998) *Prozessmanagement als Kernkompetenz – wie sie Business Reengineering strategisch nutzen können*. 2. aktualisierte und erweiterte Auflage, Wiesbaden: Gabler.
Penrose, E. (1959) *The Theory of the Growth of the Firm*. Oxford: Basil Blackwell.
Porter, M. (1980) *Competitive Strategy*. New York: Free Press.
Porter, M. (1985) *Competitive Advantage*. New York: Free Press.
Prahalad, C. K./Bettis, R. (1986) 'The Dominant Logic: A New Linkage Between Diversity and Performance'. In: *Strategic Management Journal*, 7, No. 6, 485–501.
Prahalad, C. K./Hamel, G. (1990) 'The Core Competences of the Corporation'. In: *Harvard Business Review*, May–June, 79–91.
Probst, G. (1981) *Kybernetische Gesetzeshypothesen als Basis für Gestaltungs- und Lenkungsregeln im Management*. Bern: Haupt.
Probst, G. (1987) *Selbst-Organisation*. Berlin: Parey.
Pümpin, C. (1992) *Strategische Erfolgspositionen*. Bern: Haupt.
Reckwitz, A. (1997) 'Kulturtheorie, Systemtheorie und das sozialtheoretische Muster der Innen-Aussen-Differenz'. In: *Zeitschrift für Soziologie*, 26, Heft 5, 317–36.
Reiss, M., von Rosenstiel, L./Lanz, A. (Hrsg.) (1997): *Change Management*. Stuttgart: Schäffer-Poeschel.
Rüegg-Stürm, J. (1998) 'Neuere Systemtheorie und unternehmerischer Wandel – Skizze einer systemisch-konstruktivistischen Theory of the Firm'. In: *Die Unternehmung*, 52, Heft 2, 3–17.
Rüegg-Stürm, J. (2001) *Organisation und organisationaler Wandel: eine theoretische Erkundung aus konstruktivistischer Sicht*. Opladen/ Wiesbaden: Westdeutscher Verlag.
Sackmann, S. (1991) *Cultural Knowledge in Organizations: Exploring the Collective Mind*. Newbury Park: Sage.
Sandner, K. (1992) *Prozesse der Macht: zur Entstehung, Stabilisierung und Veränderung der Macht von Akteuren in Unternehmen*. 2. Auflage, Heidelberg: Physica.
Sandner, K./Meyer, R. (1994) 'Verhandlung und Struktur: Zur Entstehung organisierten Handelns in Unternehmen'. In: Schreyögg, G./Conrad P. (Hrsg.): *Managementforschung* 4, Berlin: de Gruyter, 185–218.

Schein, E. (1985) *Organizational Culture and Leadership*. San Francisco: Jossey-Bass.

Schuh, G., Benett, S., Müller, M. and Tockenbürger, L. (1998) 'Europäisches Change-Management – von der Strategie bis zur Umsetzung prozessorientierter Organisationen'. In: *io Management-Zeitschrift*, Nr. 3, 22–9.

Schuh, G. (Hrsg.) (1999) *Change Management – von der Strategie zur Umsetzung*. Aachen: Shaker.

Schwaninger, M. (1994) *Managementsysteme*. Frankfurt: Campus.

Servatius, H.-G. (1994) *Reengineering-Programme umsetzen: Von erstarrten Strukturen zu fliessenden Prozessen*. Stuttgart: Schäffer-Poeschel.

Simon, F. (2001) *Radikale Marktwirtschaft. Grundlagen des systemischen Managements*. Heidelberg: Carl-Auer-Systeme.

Stalk, G./Hout, Th. (199/1992) *Competing Against Time: How Time-based Competition Is Reshaping Global Markets*. New York: Free Press.

Ulrich, H. (1968/1970) *Die Unternehmung als produktives soziales System*. 2. Auflage, Bern: Haupt.

Ulrich, H. (1984) *Management*. Bern: Haupt.

Ulrich, H. (1978/1987) Unternehmungspolitik. 3. durchgesehene Auflage, Bern: Haupt.

Ulrich, H./Krieg, W. (1972/1974) *St. Gallen Management-Modell*. 3. Auflage, Bern: Haupt.

Ulrich, H./Probst, G. (eds) (1984) *Self-Organization and Management of Social Systems*. Heidelberg: Springer.

Ulrich, H./Probst, G. (1988/2001) *Anleitung zum ganzheitlichen Denken und Handeln*. 4. Auflage, Bern: Haupt.

Ulrich, P. (1984) 'Systemsteuerung und Kulturentwicklung'. In: *Die Unternehmung*, 38, Heft 4, 303–25.

Ulrich, P. (1990) Symbolisches Management – ethisch-kritische Anmerkungen zur gegenwärtigen Diskussion über Unternehmenskultur. In: Lattmann (Hrsg) (1990): *Unternehmenskultur*. Heidelberg: Physica, 277–302.

Ulrich, P. (2001) *Integrative Wirtschaftsethik. Grundlagen einer lebensdienlichen Ökonomie*. 3. überarbeitete Auflage, Bern: Haupt.

Ulrich, P. (2004) 'Die normativen Grundlagen der unternehmerischen Tätigkeit'. In: Dubs, R., Euler, D., Rüegg-Stürm, J. and Wyss Ch. (Hrsg.) *Einführung in die Managementlehre*. Bern: Haupt.

Ulrich, P./Fluri, E. (1995) *Management – eine konzentrierte Einführung*. 7. Auflage, Bern: Haupt.

Walter-Busch, E. (1996) *Organisationstheorien von Weber bis Weick*. Amsterdam: Fakultas.

Watson, T. (1994) *In Search of Management. Culture, Chaos and Control in Managerial Work*. London: Routledge.

Watzlawick, P., Weakland, J. and Fisch, R. (1974): *Change. Principles of Problem Formation and Problem Resolution*. New York: W. W. Norton.

Weick, K. (1979) *The Social Psychology of Organizing*. 2nd edn, New York: McGraw-Hill.

Wenger, E. (1998) *Communities of Practice: Learning, Meaning, and Identity*. Cambridge: Cambridge University Press.

Wernerfelt, B. (1984) 'A resource based view of the firm'. In: *Strategic Management Journal*, 5, No. 2, 171–80.

Willke, H. (1996a) *Systemtheorie I: Grundlagen*. 5. überarbeitete Auflage, Stuttgart: Lucius & Lucius.

Willke, H. (1996b) *Systemtheorie II: Interventionstheorie.* 2. bearbeitete Auflage, Stuttgart: Lucius & Lucius.
Wimmer, R. (1999) 'Wider den Veränderungsoptimismus. Zu den Möglichkeiten und Grenzen einer radikalen Transformation von Organisationen'. In: *Soziale Systeme,* 5, Heft 1, 159–80.
Womack, J., Jones, D. and Roos, D. (1990) *The Machine that changed the World.* New York: Rawson Associates.

Index

Activity, 52
Activity chain, 52
Advantage of effectiveness, 11
Advantage of efficiency, 11, 36
Analytical–technical dimension, 66
Arena of change, 71

Blind spot, 5, 49
Blind work, 51
Business segmentation, 30
Business strategy, 30

Communication, 61
Communities-of-practice, 10, 77
Competencies, 33
Complexity, 2, 8
   Complex systems, 7, 8
   Reduction of, 2
Configuration, 30
Contingent, 5
Coopetition, 34
Coordination, 26
Core competencies, 33
Corporate strategy, 30
Country organisation, 37
Cultural–relational dimension, 66
Culture, 27, 43
   Corporate, 43

Depth of production, 29, 98
Differentiation, 35
Discourse, 77
Disposition, 63
Divisional organisation, 37
Dynamic systems, 8

Educational work, 61
Effectiveness, 36
Efficiency, 36
Efficiency advantages, 11, 35
Emergent, 8
Environmental spheres, 11

Financial controlling, 57
Firms, 10

Focus of value creation, 29
Functional organisation, 37
Functions, 37, 51

Infrastructure care, 61
Inside-out perspective, 33
Integration, 35
Issues, 12, 22
   Interaction, 12, 16
Information control, 61

Law, 61
Leading people, 57
Local theory, 45
Management, 11
   Model, 3
Market- or product-related areas of
   activity, 37
Market-based view, 31
Micropolitical processes of
   negotiation, 27
Models, 5
Modes of development, 13

Normative, 56
   Frame of reference, 23
   Management, 22
   Orientation processes, 56

Operative, 56
   Management processes, 57
Optimisation, 68
Organisation
   of change, 71
   country, 37
   divisional, 37
   functional, 37
   regional, 37
Organisational chart, 38
Organisational routines, 33
Organisational structure, 37
Orientation knowledge, 26
Outside-in perspective, 31
Outsourcing, 34

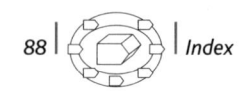

Personnel work, 61
Processes, 13, 52
   Business, 54
   CIP (Continuous Improvement Process), 63
   Core, 60
   Customer, 58
   Innovation, 60
   Management, 55
   Process architecture, 53, 54
   Process control, 53, 62
   Process development, 53, 62
   Process management, 61
   Process structures, 38
   Supply chain management, 60
   Support, 54, 60–1

Quality management, 3, 58

Range of offerings, 29
Regional organisation, 37
Renewal, 68
Resource-based view, 33
Resources, 33
Risk control, 61
Routinisation, 48

Self-referential, 46
Sense of purpose, 26, 42
Shareholder value approach, 20
Signatures, 2
Stakeholder value approach, 20
   Ethically critical, 1, 19
   Strategic stakeholder, 1, 19
Stakeholders, 12, 19
Strategic, 56
   Initiative, 30
   Management, 28
   Positioning, 23
   Strategy development processes, 57
Strategy, 26
Structuration, 10
Structures, 10, 26, 36
Structuring forces, 12, 46, 63
System, 7, 8
   Complex, 7, 8
   Dynamic, 8

Time-based competition, 51
Total value creation process, 29
Transaction costs, 34
Triage, 62

Value chain, 53, 79
Value creation chain, 79